ROADMAP TO DESTINY

**A 21-Day Devotional for Those on the Pathway
to Purpose**

Joy V. Morgan

ROADMAP TO DESTINY
Copyright © 2015 by Joy V. Morgan

Published in Burlington, NJ by MYJOY publishing
ISBN: 978-0-578-17185-2

Cover design: Final Draft Design
Printed in USA by 48HrBooks

Acknowledgements

Thank you to Glenda Vaughn for lending your time, feedback and insight to the editing process. I will be forever grateful to you for pulling the prophetic anointing out of me. Reggie Dupree of Final Draft Design, thank you for catching my vision for the book cover, you did a phenomenal job!

To my JMM staff: Words cannot describe how appreciative I am to have you on my team. To say you are absolutely priceless to me is an understatement! Brittnee, Chanel, Cherise, Katrina, Lynn, Melicia and NaKeara, thank you for your willingness to make it happen no matter what, even when it means working on a last minute request, staying up late at night, or giving of your own resources. You've more than proven that you are "with me to the end". I love you all!

To my Restoration Station family. I count it an honor and privilege to serve as one of your pastors. I appreciate your love, commitment and dedication to me, my husband and the vision of our church.

Thanks to all of my partners in the ministry who have opened up your pulpits and hearts to me. You've been a part of my roadmap to destiny, and I am grateful for our Kingdom connection.

To Bishop Jeff Poole, thank you for your spiritual covering over our ministry and personal lives. You have been such an inspiration to me personally. Whenever I hear you preach, your passion provokes me to think bigger and do all that is in my heart to do. I appreciate you sir!

To Rev. Catherine Williams, there are not enough words to express my appreciation for all that you have poured into my life spiritually throughout these past several years. The first message I ever heard you preach over a decade ago changed my life forever! Your mentoring has played a major part in where I am at this point in my journey as a wife, pastor, preacher, and mentor. I will always value the Godly wisdom and insight you

3

have imparted into my life. God knew those many years ago that to get from where I was, to where I am today, I needed you. I love you Momma Catherine!

To my sister Julia, and my sisters in law, I'm grateful for our sisterhood and love you all from the bottom of my heart.

To Norman and Bertha Morgan, I first want to thank you for giving me the gift of your only begotten son, for which I am eternally grateful!! Thank you for embracing me as your daughter and allowing me to be a part of such a wonderful, God-centered family. Your love and acceptance of me was evident from day one. I love you both dearly.

To my grandmother and to whom I owe my middle initial, thank you for showing me what it means to be a lady's lady. If I have half the class, spunk and beauty that you possess when I reach your season in life, I will be one blessed lady!! I will never take for granted your unconditional love and support. I love you Grandma!

To my parents, thank you for bringing me into the world and calling me your "joy". I remember when I was a little girl, I told you one day that I didn't like my name. All of the popular kids in school had what I perceived to be these really cool names. However, I didn't know then what I've come to realize now. God gave you my name, and it was a prophetic declaration over my life that the JOY of the Lord would always be my strength. I have experienced a lot of challenging days on this pathway to purpose, but every time my name is called, I am forced to remember that His JOY is the strength I need to see me through it all. I am the woman I am today because of your lessons, your love and your sacrifices. I love you both with all that is within me.

Finally, to my life partner, cheerleader, president of my fan club, nurse, pastor, best friend, and love of my life, Dorion Morgan. I love you more than pumpkin spice!! You are the most amazing husband a woman could ever ask for. Thank you for your love, your leadership, your covering, your provision, your protection and your promotion of me. You make me a better person. I am honored to be called your wife and privileged to bear your last name. Thank you for the gift of twenty plus years of marriage and I pray that God would give us at least fifty more! To say I love you does not begin to articulate my feelings for you, but it's the best the English language can provide...

Dedication

I dedicate this book to my Heavenly Father, my Lord and Savior Jesus Christ, and the sweet Holy Spirit. You have been my spiritual navigation system on this pathway to purpose. Without You in my life, I would be lost and devoid of direction. Thank you for anointing me to write this book, so that I might empower others to embark on their journey towards the destiny You have for them.

Table of Contents

Foreword

The life of a Christian is often very difficult. I know that's not the best sales pitch for Christianity, but the Bible declares that "Many are the afflictions of the righteous..." Then it goes on to say "... but the Lord delivers them out of them all" (Psalm 34:19). What we often fail to do is look for the Lord's deliverance. His deliverance comes by following His will for our lives. If we would just do more of what God tells us, then we would spend less time in or dwelling on our afflictions.

In my sermons, I often use the analogy of driving through a storm. When a huge storm approaches and begins to pour like a waterfall, I see many cars pulled over to the side of the road. However, I never stop and pull over. I drive as slowly as I have to and as carefully as I can, keeping my eyes on the lines on the roadway. I keep moving, which gets me out of the storm faster than if I just sat there and subjected myself to it. So many Christians just sit still in life at the mercy of the storm, when God wants them to move carefully (even slowly sometimes) towards their destiny, trusting the guiding lines that He has drawn for them. *"Thy word is a lamp unto my feet, and a light unto my path."* (Psalm 119:105, KJV)

This book will help every believer get started or restarted on their path to destiny. Pastor Joy has heard from God and has graciously shared pearls of wisdom to get us on the right track. I have personally witnessed Pastor Joy diligently seeking God on behalf of the people, even in the wee hours of the morning. Through her sacrifice, dedication and passion for God and His people, *Roadmap to Destiny* has been birthed. Without a doubt, I know this book will either motivate you into action, or redirect you to the proper path for your life, ministry, family, business, and relationship with Jesus Christ.

I encourage you to take the next twenty-one days and use this roadmap to destiny as a private motivational devotional. This power packed book of wisdom also serves as a great tool for large or small group settings with like-minded believers who are truly ready to get on their pathway to purpose.

Pastor Dorion B. Morgan, Senior Pastor
Restoration Station Christian Fellowship

Introduction

Pastor Rick Warren says in his book *The Purpose Driven Life*, "Time is your most precious gift because you only have a set amount of it. You can make more money, but you can't make more time. When you give someone your time, you are giving them a portion of your life that you'll never get back. Your time is your life."

The question is, how are you spending your time, and in essence what I'm really asking is, *how are you spending your life?*

Are you living in purpose and on purpose, or do you just simply exist? Have you ever said to yourself, "There must be more to life than THIS?"

Let's take a look at a few scriptures in the Bible to see what it has to say about purpose:

> *"Everything got started in Him and finds its purpose in Him." (Colossians 1:16b, MSG)*

> *"God has given each of you a gift from his great variety of spiritual gifts. Use them well to serve one another." (1 Peter 4:10, NLT)*

> *"Live life with a due sense of responsibility, not as those who do not know the meaning of life but as those who do." (Ephesians 5:15, J.B. Phillips)*

> *"Now when David had served God's purpose in his own generation, he fell asleep...." (Acts 13:36, NIV)*

The scriptures above indicate that God is a God of purpose and that He intends for His children to walk that purpose out towards a place called "destiny".

In the natural, *destiny*, according to the Merriam-Webster dictionary, is defined as "the inevitable or necessary fate to which a particular person or thing is destined; one's lot or a predetermined course of events considered as something beyond human power or control." This earthly definition almost seems to indicate that life is some combination of circumstances and happenstance. But that's not the kind of destiny I'm talking about. What I'm referring to is a God-given destiny as described in Jeremiah 29:11. *"For I know the thoughts that I think toward you, says the LORD, thoughts of peace and not of evil, to give you a future and a hope." (NKJV)*

God has divinely orchestrated a hope and a future for each and every one of His children, and it is our responsibility to obey His leading and follow the pathway preordained by Him from the foundations of the world.

Now practically speaking, following your pathway to purpose and destiny is easier said than done. In the reality of life, you have responsibilities that hinder you from pursuing your destiny with reckless abandon. Many of us have found ourselves caught in the web of a dead-end job or career because it pays the bills, and we feel stuck.

Perhaps that's where you are today. If so, I can relate to where you are, because I once was there too. I graduated with an undergraduate degree in Civil Engineering. Quite honestly, I knew throughout most of my college matriculation that this course of study was not for me. In actuality, I hated it. I pursued engineering because family, teachers and guidance counselors in high school thought that since I was good in math and science that the engineering curriculum would be a good fit for me. There were also a lot of scholarships being offered to women and minorities who were willing to pursue math, science and engineering, so being that I was not clear on what I really wanted to do with my life, I figured, why not? I kept hearing how I'd make a boatload of money when I came out of college with this prestigious engineering degree. So even though I despised my major, the pursuit of money was driving me to get my degree in a field that I had no desire to work in. However, I would later find out, there's more to life than money.

My college experience was one of the most challenging experiences of my life. Not just because the work was hard, but because I had no interest in what I was studying at all. But one thing I can say about myself for sure is I'm no quitter. By the time I was in my junior year of college, I was fully aware that I would not be pursuing a career in engineering, but I was in too deep to turn around at that point, and I felt that I had to finish what I started.

After I received my engineering degree, I had already started to consider what other alternatives I could pursue with this degree. So shortly after I completed my undergraduate degree, I decided to pursue my graduate degree in Higher Education Administration. While I was pursuing my graduate degree, I had the opportunity to intern at a local university's college of engineering, in which I worked on a staff that encouraged women and minorities to enter the field of math, science and engineering. At the time, I really enjoyed the work, and decided to make that my career path after I completed my graduate degree.

I initially found the work to be very rewarding, and spent several years creating special engineering programs for women and minorities, counseling with engineering students, teaching courses, etc. I was making pretty decent money and was on track to becoming one of the deans of the college, which would have been a great accomplishment for me, especially as a woman and a minority. But after a period of time, I started to find the work to be monotonous, boring, and unfulfilling.

The position that I was in had a very clearly defined ceiling. Although I was headed towards becoming a dean, it was going to take years to get there. I knew that there was much more for me than that career path could offer, and I began to fear that I would spend the rest of my life totally unfulfilled.

One day, during my time at this job, I received a card from someone with a line in it that I will never forget, because it changed my thinking and ultimately changed the course of my life. The cover of the card read, *"Success is loving what you do and doing what you love."* Up to that point in time, I attributed success to making good money. Although I was making good money, I did not feel successful because I was not walking in purpose. So I kept that card on my desk for the remainder of my time at that job to serve as a constant reminder that God was calling me out of that place of employment to pursue my dreams.

In my senior year of engineering school, I got a peek into what I was really destined for. In order to graduate, it was mandatory for every student to participate in a group engineering project. To this day, I can't tell you what the project was about. What I do recall is that my group's project had to be presented in front of a panel of professional engineers. Although I was the least knowledgeable of the content of the project in my group, they all voted that I do most of the talking about it because of my oratorical skills, which led to our group having one of the top projects in the class.

Since that time, I realized that I was gifted in public speaking, and I secretly envisioned myself as a motivational speaker and had no idea that my dream would come to pass in the form of becoming a preacher. I really did not have a good point of reference for what God was calling me to. For starters, I didn't grow up in the church as most ministers of the Gospel I had heard of, and then there was the whole issue of being a female preacher. I didn't see a whole lot of women who preached the Gospel because they were somewhat frowned upon in my Christian circle. On top of that, I had no formal ministry training, having never attended seminary. Now here I am today, a minister of the Gospel for over ten years. God truly does take the foolish things of the world to confound the wise!

It never ceases to amaze me when I get an invitation to preach at someone's church. I am the poster child for Proverbs 18:16 that says, *"A man's gift makes room for him and brings him before great men"*. My life and ministry serve as proof that your career is what you're paid for, but your calling is what you're made for.

I don't feel like I have a real blueprint for where God is taking me which is both scary and exhilarating at the same time. However, there's never a dull moment in my life! I believe there is no longer any ceiling to my destiny other than the one God or myself places upon me. The sky is the limit!

Now back to you:

I'm sure that you have enough talents, gifts and experiences to be paid to do any number of things, and call that your "career". However, just because you CAN do certain things doesn't mean that you SHOULD do them.

Many of us have acquainted our jobs with drudgery, and that's why we call it "work". We've come to accept that what we do for a living is not meant to be meaningful or fulfilling and we trade our time and energy for a mere paycheck.

If you have fallen into that mindless trap, I want you to consider that perhaps there really is more to life than what you're now experiencing in your career path, God has uniquely gifted you with skills and talents that are necessary for you to fulfill your purpose on this earth. However, you were also made to work.

I believe that you were made to have an occupation that would maximize and utilize your skills, talents, personality and life experiences. I believe that you are supposed to pursue something that really matters to you and ignites your passions in a way you never thought possible.

This type of work is better known as your "calling", the strong urge that's pushing you to accomplish great things during your lifetime. Your calling is the vocation that you were made to do. It's a job that you could work at for hours because it doesn't even feel like work, because you find it to be just that energizing and rewarding.

Now the key is to determine how to make your calling your career. Ultimately, you want to figure out a way to get paid to do what you were made to do. Remember, success is doing what you love and loving what you do. Please know that's going to be a process that will take time. First things first, you must acknowledge that you are going in the wrong direction. So if you're on the wrong track, that's okay, remember I was too. Let me serve as an example to you that it is possible to turn your life around towards destiny.

I certainly understand the woes of choosing a career at a young age. It's always been my belief that a high school senior is in no way equipped to determine the career path for the rest of their life. I also understand the pressure of joining the rat race of getting a job that will just pay the bills because we think that's what we're supposed to do. Many people grow up, go to college, get a job, support the family, retire, and then die. I've heard it said that we spend a third of our adult life working, more specifically, working at making someone else's dream come to pass. With that large amount of time spent working, shouldn't we invest it in chasing our own dreams?

I invite you to embark on a journey with me that will help lead you to your God-given destiny. Over the next 21 days, I will provide you with words of wisdom that I've gleaned from the Bible and have learned from my own personal pursuit of purpose and destiny. Your journey will begin by you first figuring out what your calling in life really is. Take some time to figure out who you really are and what you are meant to do.

Here are some questions for you to reflect on before we begin our journey:

What are you really good at doing?
What skills come naturally to you?
What are some of the things that you care about?
What kind of work would you be doing right now if you didn't have to be concerned about money?
What do people often ask for your help with?
When you're in a bad mood, what do you like to do that makes you feel better?

What could you talk about for hours and hours?
What types of facts and information do you love learning about,
even if no one pays you to do the research?

After you've answered these questions, you will probably have a good idea of what you've been created to do, which will become your roadmap to destiny. I encourage you to make it your life's mission to pursue your true purpose in life. Don't delay the journey, let's start today!

Day 1
Think Big

One day while on a plane coming home from vacation, making our descent into Philadelphia, we had gotten beneath the clouds, but we were still pretty high up in the air. As the earth came into view, I felt led to pay close attention to what I was seeing. From that particular altitude, I could only see things that were big. Cities, regions, communities, large buildings, large bodies of water, large land masses. I couldn't see small things like cars, nuances of houses, roadways and certainly not individual people. Then the Lord impressed upon my heart, "this is the earth from my view, this is my perspective. Now change your perspective. Think BIG."

What was the meaning of this revelation for me personally? I started thinking about the things God had assigned for me to do. I realized God was encouraging me to take on His perspective. See life from His view, He's looking at the BIG picture.

I was forced to ask the question, how does what I'm doing fit the big picture? Does it have the potential for a larger impact? How can what I'm currently doing impact cities, communities, regions, states, countries, and the entire world?

There was a man in the Bible by the name of Jabez who prayed a very simple prayer: *"...Oh that you would bless me and enlarge my territory! Let your hand be with me, and keep me from harm so that I will be free from pain." And God granted his request."* (1 Chronicles 4:10).

We see from this prayer, that Jabez first asks God to bless him, second he asks God to enlarge his territory or increase his responsibility. He then prays that God will be with him and stay close. Lastly, Jabez asks that God would keep him from harm so that he will be free from pain. And God granted his request.

This was a small yet effective prayer in the sight of God. Jabez understood what many people don't, that we must invite Him into our life and ask for His blessings. Jabez wanted to succeed and increase his sphere of influence for God, but He didn't want to do that apart from God. He realized if he wanted to have great influence and big success, God had to be invited into his endeavors, and God blessed his desire.

That's where those trying to build the Tower of Babel made their mistake. In Genesis chapter 11, verses 3-9, *"They said to each other, 'Come, let's make bricks and bake them thoroughly.' They used brick instead of stone, and tar for mortar."* Then they said, *"Come, let us build ourselves a city, with a tower that reaches to the heavens, so that we may make a name for ourselves; otherwise we will be scattered over the face of the whole earth."* But the Lord came down to see the city and the tower the people were building. The Lord said, *"If as one people speaking the same language they have begun to do this, then nothing they plan to do will be impossible for them. Come, let us go down and confuse their language so they will not understand each other."* So the Lord scattered them from there over all the earth, and they stopped building the city. That is why it was called Babel because there the Lord confused the language of the whole world. From there the Lord scattered them over the face of the whole earth."*

We must first recognize, the BIGNESS we seek should ultimately be to bring glory and honor to God and to make a name for Him. Our primary goal should be to have a positive impact on mankind, that the Kingdom may be expanded. If that is not the motive behind your big plans and endeavors, you risk God resisting your efforts as He did with those trying to build the tower of Babel. Proverbs 16:3 says, *"Commit thy works unto the LORD, and thy thoughts shall be established."*

Now, what does it really mean to think big? Pastor Steven Furtick put it this way, *"If your destiny isn't intimidating to you, it's probably insulting to God."* If you have something valuable in mind, a service to offer, a ministry, business, an idea to develop, or even your own raw talent to use, then you owe it to yourself, and to others to increase its scope. Why settle for anything less than the full potential of what you can do with it?

As I have discovered, thinking big requires a vision. Resources, whether it be people, finances or otherwise, are attracted to vision. You should come up with a personal vision statement for yourself, or establish a vision statement for your organization, business, ministry, or venture. A vision statement is an aspirational description of what an organization would like to achieve or accomplish in the mid-term or long-term future. It is intended to serve as a clear guide for choosing current and future courses of action. People, ministries, and businesses perish for a lack of vision.

To think big, you need to see big. If you can't see it, you won't achieve it. One thing that will help you see bigger is EXPOSURE to bigger things. Dr. Sam Chand, a leadership expert puts it this way: If all you've ever seen, is a one bedroom, one story rancher, and you're given a blank check and told you can write in whatever amount you want to build the house of your dreams, you're probably only going to build a one bedroom, one story rancher because that's all you've ever been exposed to. Exposure to bigger things is key in thinking big.

If you suspect you've been thinking too small, I also want to challenge you to think bigger by enlisting the help of others. Trying to do everything on your own will keep things small. See yourself as a small part of a greater whole, like the perspective I had on the plane. Get the help of people who are better than you in certain aspects of what you're trying to develop. Big thinkers cannot be afraid of acknowledging and accepting their own personal limitations. Gather people around you who can do what you can't do to ensure your dream grows.

Then remember, thinking big is not about you! It's your duty to society to think big. When something is potentially a real service to mankind, then it is a human duty to think and act big. Think about the impact things like mass immunization, the cell phone, and the internet have had on our society. Somebody had to think big in order for these things to come into existence.

I love the Message Bible's translation of 2 Corinthians 6:12 which states, *"The smallness you are feeling is coming from within you. Your lives are not small; you're just living them in a small way."* In other words, do not allow your vision to be compromised by the smallness that you see in your situation. I encourage you to tap into the Big One who lives on the inside of you and do not limit yourself as to what God can do in and through your life!

Unless you start vision casting for your enterprise, ministry or idea, you won't get there. Start envisioning in great detail exactly what your goal is and how your ideas will look, sound, and feel once they come to pass. I challenge you today to take some time out to pretend like your "big thing" is already in existence.

Questions for Reflection (as if you've already accomplished your goals):

What was your very first step to becoming this successful?

How did you get the initial money?

Who helped you? What are their names?

How are lives being changed and impacted?

What are people saying about your global phenomena?

What are you doing day-to-day?

Who will be working for you? What exactly will they be doing?

What color is the door of your international office?

Are you getting the BIG picture? When you can conceive it, you can receive it!

Day 2
Start Small

After you think big, you then must be willing to start small. Any major accomplishment in your life starts with one small step. Sometimes, when we consider the "big thing" we want to achieve, we can get so overwhelmed by thinking about the process to get it done, we quit before we even begin. We must remember that success is nothing more than a culmination of several small steps taken in one's pathway to destiny.

The book that you're reading right now is proof of this very fact. The truth is, at the time of this writing, I have several books in me that should have been written by now. I went to school for engineering and was required to take a technical writing class. My teacher was so impressed with my writing skills, that she asked if she could use one of my papers as a part of her text book for the next semester. It was then that the seed was planted that I had the makings of an author.

I have had complete strangers prophesy over my life that there are many books in me. I remember one of the first times this happened to me, I was in a worship service, and in the middle of the preacher's sermon, he stops in mid-sentence, as if interrupted by God Himself, and turns to me and says *"God says, write the book"* and then went right back to preaching on a totally unrelated subject. My husband just looked at me smugly as if to say, *"I told you so"*, because up to that point in time, we had countless conversations about how I should write books because of all the various things I have gone through, believing it would be a blessing to someone's life.

However, every time I even thought about writing a book, I was totally intimidated by the process. In my mind the book needed to be 1000 pages long, that encompassed every life experience I had ever encountered, and worthy to be on the best-seller's list. Then one day, God dropped this small revelation in my spirit, "start small", and that's when I decided to write this 21-day devotional. For me, it was something small, succinct, and doable.

Once I made a decision that I could do it, and I would do it, I wrote the book in only two weeks, and now I am an author!

Restoration Station, the church in which my husband and I are the founders and pastors, also began with a small start. When we actually planted the church, we started with less than ten members. But at the time of this writing, we've now been in existence for eleven years, we have had well over six-hundred members pass through our church, and countless lives have been saved, restored and changed for the better. The ministry started with a thought and a small beginning. As we were faithful to minister in the little things, God brought us more and our sphere of influence increased. Luke 16:10 states *"He who is faithful in what is least is faithful also in much; and he who is unjust in what is least is unjust also in much."*

God looks at the faithfulness of your heart in relation to how you respond to the needs of those around you. If you are faithful in ministering to the "little" people, or small groups, He will give you the "masses". World-wide ministries are not born overnight. Those who have been called to the ministry have to begin by simply touching the lives of the people around them. As it is stated in Matthew 25:21, when one is faithful with the few things that God has given them, He will make them ruler over many things and move them into larger areas of ministry.

Today's challenge is to think about the small step you can make towards your destiny. If your destiny requires you to go back to school, start researching schools on the internet that you would be interested in. If you plan to start a business, read up on how to write a business plan. If you want to write a book, purchase a book and read up on how to become an author. Just take one small step towards your destiny.

Question for Reflection:

What small step(s) can I take today towards accomplishing my God-given dream?

Day 3
Just Do It!

This slogan was coined by the shoe company, Nike in 1988. According to Wikipedia, the "Just Do It" campaign allowed Nike to go from $877 million to $9.2 billion in sales worldwide. These three simple words became one of the most highly successful marketing campaigns in American history. I believe they became so impactful to our society because of our natural propensity for procrastination. We often come up with excuses as to why we cannot or will not do what we know we've been called to accomplish.

I am reminded of the story of Jesus' first miracle in the Bible found in John 2:2-10.

> *"Now both Jesus and His disciples were invited to the wedding. And when they ran out of wine, the mother of Jesus said to Him, "They have no wine." Jesus said to her, "Woman, what does your concern have to do with Me? My hour has not yet come." 5 His mother said to the servants, "Whatever He says to you, do it."6 Now there were set there six waterpots of stone, according to the manner of purification of the Jews, containing twenty or thirty gallons apiece. Jesus said to them, "Fill the waterpots with water." And they filled them up to the brim. And He said to them, "Draw some out now, and take it to the master of the feast." And they took it. When the master of the feast had tasted the water that was made wine, and did not know where it came from (but the servants who had drawn the water knew), the master of the feast called the bridegroom. And he said to him, "Every man at the beginning sets out the good wine, and when the guests have well drunk, then the inferior. You have kept the good wine until now!"*

In essence, what Mary was saying to the disciples in verse 5 of this passage was, whatever Jesus tells you to do, "Just Do It". Nike wasn't the first one to come up with that slogan, Mary coined it a long time ago! This is good advice for us all. If the Lord drops an idea on our hearts, don't waste time trying to figure out how it will get done, where the finances will come from, what will people think of what you're doing, or what it will look like in the end, "just do it".

As we take a further look at the passage, we see first that there was a problem that presented itself in the midst of the people – there was no more wine at the wedding. We see that Mary had the faith to believe that Jesus had the answer. Now up to this point, Jesus hadn't performed any miracles yet, but she had an expectation that if the Master was in the room, He could solve the problem. So Mary's expectation became the breeding ground for a miracle to be performed that day.

In response to the problem that had presented itself, Jesus invited the disciples to partner with Him in solving that problem by telling them to fill the water pots. In other words, He was saying, if you put in the natural resource, I'll add my super to it and do the supernatural.

Jesus is still inviting His disciples to partner with Him to solve the problems that we see in the world today. This perspective helps us to take the pressure off of ourselves. As my precious mentor Rev. Catherine Williams would often remind me in the beginning stages of our ministry, we are helping Him accomplish the work, He is not helping us. Which means, that ultimately, it's His work that is to be done, and He is allowing us the opportunity to get it done. Psalm 127:1 states, *"Unless the LORD builds the house, They labor in vain who build it..."*

How do I know what problems I'm supposed to answer? You find your purpose by discovering what problem gets your attention, and figuring out what you're passionate about. It may be homelessness, hopelessness, illiteracy, or gang violence. Perhaps you feel led to provide encouragement to unwed mothers, mentor youth, strengthen women, serve as a good role model to men, help businesses that need to be started, etc.

When you determine what problem you've been called to answer, your next question may be *"Now What?"* You may feel like all you've got is an empty water pot. I join with Mary and say whatever Jesus tells you to do, just do it! Fill those pots! Do your part - write the business plan, do the research, get your non-profit status, write the introduction to the book, start finding out how to get a small business loan, do something, get started, and begin today!

Questions for Reflection:

What problem do you feel you've been called to answer?

What is hindering you from starting on the pathway to answering that problem?

What can you do in the natural to begin answering that problem?

What part is out of your control? What is it that only God can do in getting this problem answered?

Day 4
God is In the Detours

If you are anything like me, you are challenged by making decisions to the point that you do nothing. So often, we hesitate to start something because we can't see the entire journey. I want to encourage you, to take the first step, and watch God lead you to where He eventually wants you to end up. As Rev. Catherine Williams would always remind me *"you can't steer a parked car"*. If you don't take the first step, you will not give God the opportunity to steer us in the direction He wants us to go. Take the first step, and then pray "Now Jesus, take the wheel".

Now, our journey is not always going to make sense to us, but God knows exactly where He wants us to go and how He wants us to get there. We will find that on our pathway to our purpose and calling, we will encounter many detours along the way, but I have found out that God is in the detours!

My career path is a perfect example of this fact. I started out as an engineer and I am now a pastor, preacher, life coach and author. I would have never thought in a million years that my experience as an engineering major was preparing me for my calling as a pastor. The truth is, all of the things I experienced along the journey were necessary lessons that would be valuable for what I'm doing today. While I was in college for engineering, I had to learn discipline because of the rigors of this course of study. While I was at that particular university, I was invited and encouraged to join the Gospel Choir on campus. I remained in the choir throughout my college years.

While in the Gospel Choir, I came to know the Lord in a very real and meaningful way for the first time. It was there in which I fell in love with singing the praises of God and worshipping Him through song. In high school, I was a drum major for our marching band so I had experience in directing. My experience with directing the high school band, gave me the courage to audition as a director for the college Gospel Choir. I was selected as one the choir's directors, and also became a part of the choir's

26

executive team, a position which required me to manage the business of the choir and now that I look back on it I realize I was also "pastoring" the members of the choir.

While I was in college, my family had found a church home. When I returned home on one of my college breaks in between semesters, I also joined the church and soon thereafter joined one of the choirs of my church. Because of my experience as a director of my college choir, I soon became one of the directors of the church choir. And as God would have it, I met the church's organist who would eventually become my husband.

After we were married, I went on to get my Master's degree in Education Administration at a different university. As I've mentioned previously, while pursuing my master's degree, I landed a position in the School of Engineering and became a student counselor, and a director of a program that encourages young girls to pursue careers in math, science and engineering. While in this position I also had the opportunity to teach the Introduction to Engineering course to freshman students, in which I fell in love with teaching. I eventually left that position after a few years due to medical reasons, but when I was physically able to do so, I found a position as an adjunct math professor at my local county college and did that for a couple of years. Again, I had to stop teaching math for medical reasons, but I was clear on the fact that I loved to teach, motivate and inspire people to be the best that they could be, whether in math, engineering, or life in general.

After my experience as a math professor, my husband and I started a church. Initially, my husband served as the senior pastor and I was the director of operations. It wasn't long before I found myself teaching the Bible from time to time, which eventually led to my trial sermon. Soon thereafter, I was ordained as a minister of the Gospel and installed as the assistant pastor of our church.

By now, I'm sure you have connected the dots in my journey from becoming an engineer to a pastor and preacher. The pathway to my ultimate purpose was a strange and lengthy one, but God knew the path that I had to take to get to where He had predestined me to be. In the natural, this process to my destiny makes no sense, but God never wastes an experience, and as it states in Psalm 37:23, *"The steps of a good man are ordered by the Lord..."* I believe with all my heart that I had to go down this specific path with all of its seeming twists and turns, but before I was formed in my mother's womb, God had already sanctified me, and ordained me to be a messenger of God's Word. He used my experience directing the high school band and the leading the choir in college, so that I could ultimately meet my husband in the church choir. He allowed me the opportunity to teach in the college setting to realize that I'm gifted in the area of teaching and to sharpen my teaching skills so that I could eventually use them for the Kingdom's sake.

Let's not lose sight of the original point, it started with one step. As I started my journey, He steered me right in to my destiny. I never would have ended up where I am today if I never took the car out of park. Be careful not to get frustrated when you are seemingly sidetracked as you are heading towards your destiny, trust that God is in the detours!

Questions for Reflection:

What "detours" have you taken in life that seem totally unrelated to your ultimate purpose?

What lessons did you learn in those detours?

How have you been or will you be able to apply those lessons in what you have determined to be your ultimate purpose in life?

Day 5
Closed Doors are God's Divine Direction

From the time we are toddlers, humans hate to hear the word "NO". I don't know too many people that like to be denied of what they want. However, the truth of the matter is that rejection is often God's form of protection. As I heard in a sermon preached by Bishop T.D. Jakes, closed doors are a sign of divine direction. When God closes a door, it forces us to go in another direction. We must get to a place that we trust God has our best interest in mind, and He knows what's best for us. As I look back over my life, sometimes I feel like I've gotten more no's in my life than I have yes's. But I'm finally at a place in my life that I'm just as grateful for every "no" that I've received as I am for every "yes".

As a very silly example, I remember when I was in first grade, when I was about five or six years old, I had a major crush on this little boy in my class. I can remember praying each night before I went to bed that God would let this little boy and I get married. How could I think that at age six, I would understand what marriage was? I certainly couldn't know at that young age if that boy would grow up to be the kind of husband that I would want or need. I was crushed when I found out he liked another girl in the class! Why didn't God answer my prayer? Because I was an immature little girl, who had no clue what was best for me and my future.

As absurd as it was for me to be devastated that God denied my request to marry this little boy, I believe that to God, some of my prayer requests as a grown woman are just as ridiculous as this little girl's prayer. Jeremiah 29:11 (NIV) says *"For I know the plans I have for you," declares the LORD, "plans to prosper you and not to harm you, plans to give you hope and a future"*. Since His plans are to prosper us and not to harm us, He often has to close doors so that He can shield us from what is behind those doors.

There have been seasons in my life when every door I tried to open was shut right in my face, and I was left with only one option. Sometimes that only option came in the form of "stand still" or "wait". At other times, it came in the form of me having to blaze a trail that was never there before. I truly believe there would be no Restoration Station if my husband and I had not encountered one particular closed door in our lives.

At some point, the Lord led me and my husband to leave the church in which we met. My husband was born and raised in that church and it was my first church home. It was not an easy decision, but we knew we had to obey God. That church had been around for over one hundred years and was very well established in the community with a rich heritage. After leaving that church, of all places, God led us to a church that had just started meeting in the pastor's basement. What a stark difference from what we had just come from!

However, it was there we gained new insight into the ways of God, introduced to the power of praise and worship, and experienced the Holy Spirit like we had never encountered Him before. The pastor was a gifted and anointed teacher of the Word and was very skilled at presenting Biblical principles in an enlightening way. The church eventually grew out of the pastor's basement, and we began to have worship services in a school auditorium. Services were packed, and attendance had gotten up to approximately one hundred people per service.

My husband soon became the minister of music, and I eventually became the worship leader, which turned into a real passion for me. We gained a lot of ministry experience there, and we were exposed to another facet of the Kingdom of God that we had never known. My husband also accepted his call to the ministry during that time and preached his initial sermon at that church. But unfortunately, at some point, the church encountered some major bumps in the road. Consequently, the membership began to dwindle such that the remaining members were forced to worship back in the pastor's basement where we initially started.

Due to the sporadic attendance of the few members that were left, services were held on an inconsistent basis. One day, my husband and I showed up for service, and when we got to the house, the door was closed and locked with a sign on the door, "There will be no service today". The church never held a regular worship service after that point. We found ourselves in the presence of a "closed door". *Now what?* After what we had experienced in God during our short time at this church, we felt like we couldn't go back to the church prior to this one, and we didn't have direction as to where to go.

Once the word got out that we were in need of a church home again, my husband was offered a few minister of music positions, but there was no place of worship that felt like a fit for us. We finally realized that God was leading us to start a church. However, my husband had only preached two sermons and was not yet ordained up to that point. My husband had no real preaching experience and we certainly didn't know much about church planting other than what we observed during our time at this last church. Nevertheless, after much prayer and contemplation, we were quite clear that it was God's will that we start a church, which would become "Restoration Station Christian Fellowship", the result of a closed door.

I am now in the habit of praying, *"open doors that no man can shut, and shut doors no man can open."* I shudder to think about all of the lives that would NOT have been touched and impacted by our ministry had we not encountered a "closed door". God knew before we ever encountered the church in the basement, that it had an expiration date. It was just the "boot camp" as I've come to call it, that we needed to start our ministry. Had we not been exposed to a church plant, we would have never even conceived of the idea of starting a church. God does all things well. As Bishop Jakes so eloquently stated in the aforementioned sermon, *"the absence of options is truly the presence of direction"*.

I challenge you today to stop trying to bang down a door that the Lord has clearly closed. Let it go, and consider what God may be trying to do with and through you in the absence of other options. It may be bigger than the opportunity you were seeking after. That job that let you go may be the start of your business. That boyfriend or girlfriend that broke up with you may lead you to finding your spouse. Change your perspective concerning the closed doors in your life. Instead, rejoice, believing that God must have something greater in store for your life. The famous country singer Garth Brooks put it this way, *"Some of God's greatest gifts are unanswered prayers."*

Questions for Reflection:

What are some of the closed doors you've encountered in your life?

Up to this point, how have you handled closed doors?

How will you now handle closed doors as you progress in your journey towards destiny?

Looking back at some of those closed doors, can you identify how they were used by God to steer you where He ultimately wanted you to be?

Day 6
Fly Above Your Fear of Failure

On our quest for success, our biggest fear is often the fear of failure. This fear has the potential to paralyze us into inaction, causing us to never reach our God ordained destinations. What I've learned over the years is that you cannot conquer what you won't confront. Today, I want to encourage you to face the fear of failure and my prayer is that you will not only face it, but fly above it.

The Bible states in 1 John 4:18 (NKJV) *"There is no fear in love; but perfect love casts out fear, because fear involves torment. But he who fears has not been made perfect in love."* Fear is an unpleasant emotion caused by the belief that someone or something is dangerous, and is likely to cause pain or a threat. Torment is defined as severe physical or mental suffering. It is not the will of the Father that we would live a life filled with the perceived threat of danger in conjunction with unbearable suffering mentally or physically. Since 1 John 4:8 tells us God is love, 1 John 4:18 is really saying, God casts out all fear. Therefore, we must bask in the perfect love of God that is sure to deliver us from the bondage caused by fear.

Worry often accompanies fear. In Ed Young's book *Outrageous, Contagious Joy*, he defines worry as *"an inordinate amount of anxiety about something that is probably not going to happen."* Psalm 23:4 says, *"Yea, though I walk through the valley of the SHADOW (emphasis mine) of death, I will fear no evil, for You are with me..."* We must realize that a shadow has no power, and we often fear what is only a shadow of death, trouble, or failure. The SHADOW of a gun can't kill you, the SHADOW of a negative doctor's report can't kill you, and the SHADOW of failure can't destroy you, because it's only a SHADOW!

We shouldn't allow ourselves to be tormented by the shadows of life as we pursue our purpose. However, we must remember the acronym for F.E.A.R. - False Evidence Appearing Real. Be encouraged by Psalms 91:5-7 (NKJV) that says, *"You shall not be afraid of the terror by night, Nor of the arrow that flies by day, Nor of the pestilence that walks in darkness, Nor of the destruction that lays waste at noonday. A thousand may fall at your side, and ten thousand at your right hand; But it shall not come near you."*

I've heard financial guru Dave Ramsey say, *"You fear things in proportion to your ignorance of them".* The enemy dwells in ignorance, giving him more territory to operate in. Your ignorance is the strength of your enemy.

A dear pastor friend of mine, Pastor Ronnie Smith, and I shared a mutual fear of flying. He has since gone on to be with the Lord, but we'd talk about our fear of flying every time we'd see each other. He lived in Bermuda and after my flight over to the island he'd ask how I handled the flight. One day, he revealed what had finally helped ease his fear of flying. He had thoroughly researched airplanes, from how they are built, how they take off, how they stay in the air, to how they land. When you become more knowledgeable of the thing you are afraid of, it eases your fears.

I heard a similar testimony in a video from Tyler Perry, entitled *"Flying Above Your Fear"*, in which he shared his fear of flying and how it began to hinder his work. Like my friend Pastor Ronnie, he researched planes, overcame his fears, and now is a pilot and flies himself around the world to his various destinations. How's that for conquering fear? When you confront what makes you afraid, you discover that freedom lies on the other side of fear.

What you also need to understand is that fear is a spirit, and that spirit is not of God. *"For God has not given us a spirit of fear, but of power and of love and of a sound mind"* (2 Timothy 1:7, NKJV).

In the book entitled *It* written by Craig Groeschel, he says that those individuals and ministries that have the "it factor" aren't afraid to fail, stating:

"Those with it take risks and at first glance don't appear to succeed. They fail often. But when they do fail, they tend to rebound quickly. Temporary failures are often followed by lasting success. They try, fail, learn, adjust, and try again. After a series of accidental learning experiences, these hard-hitting leaders often stumble onto innovative ministry ideas they never would have discovered with-out rolling the dice. As John Dewey once said, "Failure is instructive. The person who really thinks, learns quite as much from his failures as from his successes."

Walter Brunell puts it this way, *"failure is the tuition you pay for success."* I've also heard it said that your best teacher is your last mistake. Therefore, we should change our perspective on failure. Failure can work in your favor, so there is no longer any need to fear it.

I've been a praise and worship leader for years. When my pastor first asked me to serve as the worship leader of our church, I was scared to death! I feared messing up the song by forgetting the words or going off tune. However, I decided to *"do it afraid"*, in the words of Joyce Meyer. Lo and behold, one day while leading worship, I messed up! I stumbled over the words, and as embarrassed as I was, I kept going. It was then that I realized that even when you mess up, the song goes on. I got the revelation that my job is to get the congregation to worship God, not listen to me. When I realized it wasn't about me, I realized it didn't matter if I messed up, because it's not about me, it's all about Him!

Let me also add, you must learn to laugh at yourself - don't take yourself too seriously! When I sing the wrong notes while leading worship, I will often turn to my praise team, smile and we'll laugh together. In so doing, I take the enemy's power away to provoke fear and consequently paralyze me from getting up and leading worship again. I've learned to laugh at myself before he does!

I'll never forget one particular service in which I was leading worship. During one of the songs, one of my praise team members whispered to me, "*Sit down.*" I was bewildered as to why she would ask me to have a seat while I'm in the middle of leading a song. Now meanwhile, as I was singing, I did feel wind blowing through my legs, but figured that it was just the fresh wind of the Holy Spirit, however, not so! Would you believe my skirt had fallen all the way down to my ankles, and I hadn't even realized it? There I was, in all of my glory, standing there in just my suit jacket, no slip on, with my bare legs in front of the entire congregation! You know what I did once I finally heeded my praise team member's advice to sit down? I started cracking up, hysterically! I'm so glad that I had learned by that point not to take myself too seriously.

So the next time you think about allowing the fear of failure to stop you from doing what God has called you to do, think about my skirt around my ankles. The moral of the story is, I survived! And you will too. Embarrassing moments like mine may happen. You may encounter obstacles or mess up along the way, but as I stated earlier, the song will go on!

I want you to ask God, right now, to give you the courage to overcome your worst fears. Courage is strength in the face of fear. Do it afraid, and watch yourself fail forward to your destiny!

Questions for Reflection:

What would you do in life if you weren't afraid of failing at it?

What are your worst fears concerning the pursuit of your destiny? Write them down.

What would be your contingency plans if those fears were realized?

Chapter 7
Don't Let the Haters Halt You

Everyone is not going to be excited about your decision to pursue your calling. Unfortunately, you may have to face opposition from people along your pathway to purpose. No one wants to be rejected, and so often, the fear of rejection is often more tormenting than the actual act of being rejected.

The reality is, if you do anything, you are going to be the object of criticism. It is easy to be discouraged by the negative opinions of others. Like the fear of failure, the fear of criticism can paralyze you. Nevertheless, don't let the haters halt you!

The Urban dictionary defines a hater as:

> *"1. A person that simply cannot be happy for another person's success or a person who feels anger and/or jealousy for someone who has succeeded in something they have worked hard for. 2. A being who speaks badly, and/or takes negative actions in attempt to create problems for a successful person". 3. A label applied to people who are more negative than positive when discussing another person. It most commonly refers to individuals whose negativity is so extreme that it is all-consuming. However, there are various levels and forms of being a hater, ranging from completely dismissing any positive traits or actions, to merely painting a less than flattering picture by using words with negative connotations. Hating is often attributed to jealousy, but just as often, it seems to stem from some other source."*

"Hating" on someone is not exactly the same as jealousy. Rather than being happy about the accomplishments of another person, haters make a point of exposing a flaw in that person. The hater doesn't really want to be the person he or she "hates", but rather the hater wants to knock someone else down a notch in the eyes of other people.

We must realize that the real hater is the devil. He is the accuser of the brethren and the father of lies. He's jealous because we took his place with the Father. He knows his ultimate demise is coming, so in the meantime, he's trying to make as many of God's people miserable as possible. Consequently, he influences people all the time - Christians, so called friends, and even family. He will use anyone to discourage you from pursuing your God-given destiny.

As you come against haters, keep the following things in mind. One, recognize everyone's not going to like you or support your dreams. You must be healed from the "disease to please" and delivered from approval addiction. That's why as you embark on your journey to achieving your goals, you must be convinced that you've heard from God for He will be your greatest supporter.

Also, don't let negative comments and criticism distract you or keep you from what you've been called to do. Don't worry about people who talk about you behind your back, they are BEHIND you for a reason. Therefore stay focused, and realize some negative comments about you or what you're doing aren't even worth a response. Jesus serves as a great example as to how we should handle our haters.

Matthew 27:11-13 says:

> And Jesus stood before the governor: and the governor asked him, saying, Art thou the King of the Jews? And Jesus said unto him, Thou sayest. And when he was accused of the chief priests and elders, he answered nothing. Then said Pilate unto him, Hearest thou not how many things they witness against thee? And he answered him to never a word; insomuch that the governor marveled greatly.

The lesson we learn from this passage is that there are times when we shouldn't even waste our energy on responding to negativity and criticism. Sometimes the best response, is no response.

Stop trying to convince the people who are against you to like you. Take that energy you may be tempted to use on your enemies and pour it into working on your dream. The Bible teaches that you shouldn't even try to change their minds about you. Proverbs 26:4 (KJV) states, *"when arguing with fools, don't answer their foolish arguments, or you will become as foolish as they are"*. Matthew 7:6 (NKJV) says *"Do not give what is holy to the dogs; nor cast your pearls before swine, lest they trample them under their feet, and turn and tear you in pieces."*

Although you should not spend valuable time arguing with your enemies, I encourage you to hear what God may be trying to say to you through them. Sometimes, the Lord will use the mouth of your haters to prophecy to you about your future.

Exodus 2:11-14

Now it came to pass in those days, when Moses was grown, that he went out to his brethren and looked at their burdens. And he saw an Egyptian beating a Hebrew, one of his brethren. So he looked this way and that way, and when he saw no one, he killed the Egyptian and hid him in the sand. And when he went out the second day, behold, two Hebrew men were fighting, and he said to the one who did the wrong, "Why are you striking your companion?" Then he said, "Who made you a prince and a judge over us? Do you intend to kill me as you killed the Egyptian?" So Moses feared and said, "Surely this thing is known!"

The irony of this story is that Moses eventually did become prince. God was using the one in the wrong to foretell his future. I heard Bishop T.D. Jakes once say that the hatred of your enemy helps to tutor you in your own significance. So listen closely, your haters just may have a prophetic word for you!

Lastly, I want to encourage you to always take the high road concerning your haters. Keep in mind the words of Jesus in Matthew 5:44. *"But I say unto you, Love your enemies, bless them that curse you, do good to them that hate you, and pray for them which despitefully use you, and persecute you."* Your enemies are not worth the risk of getting in trouble with God because you've decided to take retaliation into your own hands. *"Vengeance is mine saith the Lord, I will repay"* (Romans 12:19, KJV). I know it may be easier said than done, but you can do all things through Christ who strengthens you! (Philippians 4:13)

Questions for Reflection:

Do you have a fear of rejection?

Can you identify the haters in your life?

Have your haters had an impact on your pursuit of destiny?

If so, how have you treated them up to this point?

How will you treat them as a result of what you've just read?

Chapter 8
Find the Right Travel Partners

Relationships are vital while on your journey to accomplishing your dreams and aspirations. Your friends can help get you to your destiny or hinder you from making it to your destiny. The Bible says in Proverbs 1:20 (KJV), *"He that walketh with wise men shall be wise: but a companion of fools shall be destroyed."* Therefore, you must be intentional about selecting your travel partners on the road to destiny.

This revelation changed the course of my life. When I first accepted my calling as a pastor and preacher, I had to make the difficult decision to distance myself from those who were not going in the same direction as I was. On the other hand, I became very deliberate in bringing certain people into my sphere of influence. I can still remember the day, over ten years ago, in which I asked Rev. Catherine Williams to be my spiritual mentor. I found it very intimidating to ask her to mentor me because I didn't think that someone at her level of ministry and spiritual maturity would have time for what I perceived to be "little ol' me". To my surprise, she graciously accepted the responsibility, and I know our relationship was instrumental in ushering me into the next level of my ministry.

Are you frustrated with your lack of progress, are you not moving forward? Perhaps you should look around you. I've heard it said that the contacts in your cell phone can reveal who you are, where you're going and how much money you make. The point is that you become who you surround yourself with. The old adage says, *"Birds of a feather, flock together."*

Jesus had people around Him all the time. I will place them in the following categories: the Crowd, His Colleagues, the Committed, and His Confidants. While pursuing your destiny, all four categories have their place and level of significance, but it is imperative that you know the difference as to who fits in which category in your life.

The crowd can be defined as those acquaintances who are on the fringes of your life. These are people you may see occasionally, but are loosely connected with. In the life of Jesus, the crowd was often referred to as the multitudes. He ministered to them, but He had no real relationship with them.

Colleagues are associates, those with whom you have a working relationship. Jesus' colleagues would be considered the seventy as mentioned in Luke 10:1-24. He appointed them and sent them out to go before Him to every city and place that He was about to go to prepare the crowds for His coming. The seventy worked for and with Jesus, serving as what we would call today His marketing agents.

The committed people in your life are those you would consider friends or travel partners on the path to destiny. You have a deeper relationship with your friends than the crowd or your colleagues, because you share a special bond of affection. In a friendship, there should be a mutual respect for each other's time, convictions, and goals. The twelve disciples would be considered Jesus' committed circle of people or travel partners. They supported His mission, shared His beliefs and sacrificed their lives for His cause.

Finally, there are confidants, those who you would categorize as your best friends. This is an exclusive set of travel partners that go where some of the other friends can't and won't go. You share your secrets with them, trusting that they will not be repeated to others. Peter, James and John could be considered Jesus' confidants. When He went up to the Mount of Transfiguration in Matthew Chapter 17:1-9, He only took these three disciples. This is where He was elevated and commended by God the Father. Also, when Jesus went to the Garden of Gethsemane right before He was to be crucified as mentioned in Matthew 26:36-46, He again took only Peter, James and John. In this garden, He allowed Himself to be vulnerable in the presence of this inner circle. It was there in which He asked for their prayers and support as He faced the most challenging time in His life.

In both scenarios, it is revealed that His confidants were not perfect, but Jesus trusted them because of their deep love for Him. On the Mount of Transfiguration, Peter made the mistake of wanting to put Jesus on equal footing with Elijah and Moses who had appeared during the transfiguration. Peter suggested that the disciples make three tabernacles, one for Jesus, Elijah and Moses. But while Peter was still speaking, God spoke from Heaven and turned their attention to Jesus only, saying *"This is my beloved Son, in whom I am well pleased."*

In the Garden of Gethsemane, Jesus asked the disciples to watch and pray with Him as He prepared for the agony of the cross. However, when He came to the disciples on two occasions, He found them sleep, provoking Him to ask them the question, *"Can you not pray with me for one hour?"* Your inner circle may miss the mark sometimes, but if they love you unconditionally, and can otherwise be trusted with your successes, secrets and vulnerabilities, be gracious and merciful as they make mistakes along this journey with you.

Our future is determined by the people we call our friends and confidants because we often align our lives with them. Due to their proximity, they have access to our ear gates, so their words carry weight, and we are therefore susceptible to their influence. If your friends are going in the same direction as you are, and have the same morals and beliefs as you, their influence isn't problematic. But if they do not share your core values and beliefs, and are not on board with your goals and aspirations, they can deter you from your destiny.

Let's examine the criteria Jesus used for friendship in John 15:13-16 (NKJV):

> *"Greater love has no one than this: to lay down one's life for one's friends. You are my friends if you do what I command. I no longer call you servants, because a servant does not know his master's business. Instead, I have called you friends, for everything that I learned from my Father I have made known to you. You did not*

choose me, but I chose you and appointed you so that you might go and bear fruit—fruit that will last—and so that whatever you ask in my name the Father will give you".

From this passage, we see in verse 13 that your friends are willing to lay down their life for you. Even if your friends are not willing to die for you physically, they should be willing to be inconvenienced on your behalf. They should be willing to sacrifice their time, energy or resources for your benefit. Bottom line, those who you consider friends should add value to your life and be ready to go above and beyond for you. Your key relationships should be supportive, positive and encouraging.

In verse 14, Jesus indicates that His friends do whatever He commands. I'm not trying to convey that our friends should follow OUR commands, but rather heed the commandments of Jesus. They should live in a Godly manner that represents Christ and His Kingdom well.

In verse 15, whatever the Father communicated with Jesus, He shared with His friends. The more information you share with someone, the more intimate the relationship. Sometimes, we share intimate details of our life with people too fast, and consequently entangle ourselves in what we later realize are unhealthy relationships. When someone knows our personal secrets, we don't feel we can get out of the relationship, for fear they may betray our trust. Therefore, it is important that your inner circle can be trusted with personal information.

Finally, we see in verse 16, that Jesus chose His friends. You too should choose who's in your inner circle. Don't allow people entrance into your personal space without your permission. Although you can't choose your family, as adults you can choose their proximity and how much access you give them to your ear gates.

On a practical level, I would like to share the following criteria I believe you should use in choosing your friends, or travel partners (I will be using these terms interchangeably from this point forward). For starters, they should have their own personal walk with God. Their commitment to Christ should come before their commitment to you so that they can help guard you against immoral traps set by the devil. Your friends shouldn't empower your dysfunction nor justify your weaknesses. Just because your inner circle is a support system doesn't mean it is a fan club. The people you lend your ear to should care enough to tell you when you're drifting off course. In Ecclesiastes 4:9-10 (KJV) says, *"Two are better than one; because they have a good reward for their labour. For if they fall, the one will lift up his fellow: but woe to him that is alone when he falleth; for he hath not another to help him up."*

Your travel partners should help you think bigger and should include people that are further along than you in their pursuit of their dreams. You should not be the smartest person in your sphere of influence. We are like fish, who grow to the proportion of the tank that they live in. We shouldn't be content to be a big fish in a small pond.

Your friends should challenge you to change. When you leave their presence, you should feel a sense of inadequacy that makes you want to be and do better. Your sphere of influence should put a demand on you to be all that you are supposed to be in God. Being comfortable will keep you complacent and will not allow you to reach your God-given destiny. But even in their constructive criticism, you should be able to trust that they have your best interest at heart. Iron sharpens iron, as stated in Proverbs 27:17, but it shouldn't cut.

Your travel partners should also share your core values of integrity, excellence, perseverance, and hard work. They should be made up of people who are constantly moving forward, checking off goals as they've been reached, and mapping out new strategies. They should be individuals who aren't satisfied with the status quo, but rather challenge the way in which things are done, always looking for ways to improve upon themselves.

Your travel partners should be able to discern when you're tired *in* the work not *of* the work, and encourage you accordingly. They must realize that sometimes you're going to say things out of frustration that you really don't mean. You need people around you who will pour back into you when you've emptied yourself out to the point of depletion.

While you are in fervent pursuit of your destiny, you need spiritual midwives, people who are going to help you birth what's inside of you. Be sure to surround yourself with dream catchers, not dream killers. People like Nathan who said to David in 1 Chronicles 17:2 (NKJV), *"Do all that's in your heart, for God is with you."* Your travel partners should be for you, not in competition with you.

On a final note, I can't stress enough how you should guard yourself and use wisdom when bringing people into your life. Remember, those you align yourself with will ultimately help shape your future. Choose wisely and ask God for discernment.

Questions for Reflection:

Have you placed the people in your life in the right categories — the crowd, colleagues, committed and confidants?

Are there people you should distance from your sphere of influence?

Can you identify the names of those who are your friends or travel partners?

Who would you consider to be your confidants?

Is the Lord impressing upon your heart to invite certain people into your inner circle?

Day 9
Play the Hand That You've Been Dealt

I used to love to play the card game of spades. I actually met my husband over a spades table. We started out on opposite teams, but when my spades partner and I beat him and his partner unmercifully, he decided he never wanted to be on an opposing team against me again. Consequently, he asked me to be his spades partner during the next game, and 20 years later we've been partners in spades and life ever since. Just as a disclaimer, my husband may not agree with the historical content of this story, but since I am the one who's doing the writing, I get to tell the story my way!

In any case, there have been times when the cards have been dealt in a particular game I'm playing and my hand is horrible. In those times, my immediate thought is, *"we're going to lose this hand."* Unfortunately, you can't control how the cards get dealt. In spades, you're hoping for a hand full of high trump cards, such as the ace and king of spades, and if you play like me, the big and little jokers. Even the aces and kings in other suits will work well to turn books. However, there are times when you may get a bad handful of low cards in suits other than spades, like the two of hearts and two of clubs.

However, here's what I found out in the card game of life according to Romans 8:28, *"And we know that all things work together for good to them that love God, to them who are the called according to [his] purpose."* I've also learned from 1 Thessalonians 5:18 (KJV), *"In everything give thanks: for this is the will of God in Christ Jesus concerning you"*.

Having great cards increases the chances of winning the hand, but it really doesn't guarantee victory just like having a less than desirable hand doesn't mean defeat. There are other factors that go into winning a card game. The hand that you have been dealt cannot be changed, but the way you play it can.

I want to refer to some material that Pastor Rick Warren taught when he was on *"Oprah's Lifeclass"*. Pastor Rick stated that *"Life is like a game of poker."* Now I've been talking about spades, but the principle is the same, you have to play the hand you're dealt.

According to Pastor Rick the first card is your Chemistry or Biology. He stated that *"We are all intentionally flawed to make us unique. ... You need to reframe everything you think is a flaw in life as a mark of uniqueness."* Therefore, don't look at your scars, weight, height, looks and health issues that you were born with in a negative light. Instead, see them as signs of your uniqueness.

Pastor Rick referred to the second card as "Connections", in other words, your relationships. He says, *"We were wired to be connected to each other. We're made for relationships."* We were born into many of our relationships, and some of those relationships, such as friendships and marriages, transpired along life's journey.

He refers to the third card as "Circumstances", the things that life throws at you or the things that are done to you, both good and bad. He says, *"We give the third card way too much power."* As I'm sure you have already experienced, things in life happen, such as divorce, the death of a loved one, sickness, and financial issues.

At age 18, I was diagnosed with Crohn's disease, which can be a debilitating condition of the digestive system filled with painful episodes of flare ups to include, intestinal blockages, high fevers, inflammation of the joints, anorexia, and a host of other uncomfortable and potentially life-threatening symptoms. I've had my share of hospital stays to include bowel surgeries, and have had to take lots of pills on a daily basis. It was a blow to me when I was initially diagnosed, which leads me to Pastor Rick's next card.

The fourth card is "Consciousness", the story you tell yourself. As Pastor Rick put it, *"You have to change your autopilot talk. The way you think affects the way you feel and the way you feel affects the way you act."* You may have heard it said that life is 10 percent what happens to you and 90 percent how we react to it. Your attitude affects your altitude in life.

Therefore, I had to decide that Crohn's Disease will not define me nor will it limit or determine my success in life. I made a choice to use this test as my testimony, this mess as my message, and it has become a platform for my ministry. I get to demonstrate to the world that even in adversity, God still has a plan for your life. If you have been dealt a bad hand, be encouraged, because your setback is a setup for God to use you for His glory.

Pastor Rick refers to the fifth card as "Choices", and says that this is the wild card. He states, *"This can change the suit and number or any card...One of the greatest gifts God gave us (besides Jesus Christ) is the gift of free choice. This card truly can win or lose the game."*

On the same *"Oprah's Lifeclass"* that featured Pastor Rick, a guest by the name of Nick Vujicic was also on the show. Nick was born with no arms and no legs. At age 10, he attempted suicide because he thought his life was hopeless and void of purpose, but then one day, he made a conscious choice to "think outside the box." Nick stated *"It's all about choices. I had parents who were my heroes. They always said you can either be angry for what you don't have or be thankful for what you do have. Do your best and God will do the rest."*

With no arms or legs, he golfs, surfs, plays the drums, is married, and has two children. God has truly used his life as an example to the world, that if we play the hand that we've been dealt to the best of our ability, we can still win the game of life.

What I like about spades, is that it's a team oriented game. Just when I think there's no way we can win because all I have is one or 2 good books in my hand, my husband will encourage me with his famous line, *"That's why you've got a partner"*, and to my surprise and relief he'll say I've got 4 or 5 books." I can then breathe a sigh of relief because we still have a chance at winning the game because my partner is able to make up the difference in what I did not have in my hand.

The point is, you're not in this journey alone. God is your partner, and He's got what you need to win. He knows the hand that you've been dealt, and He likes to confound the wise by allowing those who look like they've got a losing hand to come out on top.

I'm sure that you have experienced trials and hardships. If you haven't yet, keep on living, for life's challenges are sure to come. I know that you may have been dealt some tough hands from time to time, but with God on your side, you can play the hand you've been dealt successfully, and win the card game of life.

Questions for Reflection:

What bad "cards" have you been dealt in life?

Since you can't change those cards, how are you going to play them?

Are you going to fold or proceed in a timid manner?

Are you going to accept them and still move forward towards your goals?

Will you blame your cards for your misfortune for most of your life?

How will you partner with God and play to win?

Day 10
Discernment is Your Key to Possession

The word "discern" means to exercise judgement. Discernment is the art of knowing when it is God acting upon or speaking to us, and when it is not. Someone who knows what God is like, knows what His voice is like. However, what is discerned must be consistent with what God has said previously. To grow in discernment, we must work at it, like prayer, and other aspects of our spiritual life. We must be committed to learning when it was the Lord speaking in our lives and when it is not.

1 Samuel 3:1-10

> *Now the boy Samuel ministered to the LORD before Eli. And the word of the LORD was rare in those days; there was no widespread revelation. And it came to pass at that time, while Eli was lying down in his place, and when his eyes had begun to grow so dim that he could not see, and before the lamp of God went out in the tabernacle of the LORD where the ark of God was, and while Samuel was lying down, that the LORD called Samuel. And he answered, "Here I am!" So he ran to Eli and said, "Here I am, for you called me. And he said, "I did not call; lie down again." And he went and lay down. Then the LORD called yet again, "Samuel!" So Samuel arose and went to Eli, and said, "Here I am, for you called me." He answered, "I did not call, my son; lie down again." ⁷ (Now Samuel did not yet know the LORD, nor was the word of the LORD yet revealed to him.) And the LORD called Samuel again the third time. So he arose and went to Eli, and said, "Here I am, for you did call me." Then Eli perceived that the LORD had called the boy. Therefore Eli said to Samuel, "Go, lie down; and it shall be, if He calls you, that you must say, 'Speak, LORD, for Your servant hears.'" So Samuel went and lay down in his place. Now the LORD came and stood and called as at other times, "Samuel! Samuel!" And Samuel answered, "Speak, for Your servant hears."*

We too are living in a day in which the Word of the Lord is rare, even in a time when Bibles are available in abundance, Christian radio and television can be heard and seen worldwide, and there are churches on almost every corner of every city. So why is the Word of God so scarce when it is so abundantly available? It's not that God isn't speaking, we just aren't listening.

In John 10:2-5 (NIV) it says:

> *The man who enters by the gate is the shepherd of his sheep. The watchman opens the gate for him, and the sheep listen to his voice. He calls his own sheep by name and leads them out. When he has brought out all his own, he goes on ahead of them, and his sheep follow him because they know his voice. But they will never follow a stranger; in fact, they will run away from him because they do not recognize a stranger's voice.*

I once read that in Palestine, shepherds walk ahead of their sheep. Even if the sheep mix with other sheep at a waterhole, the shepherd can separate his own sheep by just calling out to them. They know the voice of their shepherd and follow him. A tourist in Palestine once asked a shepherd whether the sheep would ever follow anyone else. The shepherd replied, *"Yes, when they are sick they will follow anyone."*

I believe that we are living in a day, where many of God's sheep are "sick" and following voices other than the Voice of God. The Bible states in Matthew 24:24 (NLT), *"for false messiahs and false prophets will rise up and perform great signs and wonders so as to deceive, if possible, even God's chosen ones."* Therefore, we must be able to sharpen our ability to discern the voice of God from all other competing voices, including our own, so that we do not get sidetracked or detoured while on the road towards our destiny.

In 1 Samuel chapter 3, Samuel was performing his usual religious duties and God began to call out to him. God chose to speak to Samuel because He had plans to do a new thing through him. God is calling out to you as well, as He wants to do a new thing through you, and take you to a new place, to do things in a new way. The Lord has a pre-ordained destiny for you, your family and your community, and He is calling out to you to do it.

We need to press into the presence of God to hear His voice, so we must be intentional about spending time in church, prayer, and praise. However, we can be in the presence of God, and still miss the voice of God like Samuel.

Why didn't Samuel know the voice of God? In verse 7, it says *"Now Samuel did not yet know the LORD: The word of the LORD had not yet been revealed to him"*. Samuel was a boy. His knowledge of God was limited because he was a child. He did not yet have the kind of relationship with God that he would later have the rest of his life. Therefore, when God called to him, Samuel was unable to hear and recognize God's call.

God is challenging us in our pursuit of destiny to grow up and mature so that we might know His voice and distinguish it from others, including our own. He speaks to us through circumstances, reading the Bible, the preached Word of God or sometimes in a still small voice. In any case, it is imperative that we know God's voice on the pathway to purpose, because if we don't, it could have life-altering results, as I have personally experienced.

Several years ago, I experienced a really bad flare-up of the Crohn's Disease which landed me in the hospital. I had a hole in my transverse colon, which led to the formation of an abscess, resulting in a dangerously high fever and other potentially life-threatening symptoms. The attending gastroenterologist informed me that I would need a bowel resection to cut out the section of the colon with the hole in it. He assured me that the surgeon would only need to remove a small section of the bowel, and if a colostomy bag was needed, it would only be on a temporary basis. I certainly was not thrilled about the prospect of surgery, or a colostomy bag, even if it was only for a short period of time. However, I realized that my condition was life-threatening so I mentally prepared myself for what needed to be done.

Just as I was embracing my fate, my attending doctor's boss, who was the top gastroenterologist in the hospital, came in my hospital room to see me. I'll never forget him sitting next to me on the bed, looking me in the eye and saying, *"we've decided to remove your entire colon."*

I was absolutely shocked and bewildered by this new decision. I asked why the change in approach to this surgery and he replied that if they took out the entire colon, I would never have to worry about Crohn's Disease again (which I later found out from another doctor is absolutely NOT true). At age 34, I was being sentenced to wearing a bag in the place of my intestines for the rest of my life, which would be totally life-altering; I was not comfortable with that decision, at all!

After much prayer and deliberation, my husband and I decided to get a second opinion, so we asked to be released from the hospital, against medical advice. Needless to say, my doctors were not in agreement with that decision, but we felt a strong leading of the Lord that I should leave and admit myself into another hospital that had some of the top gastroenterologists in the country.

When I arrived, my new doctors reviewed my records, and they were in disbelief that my other doctors had proposed that my entire colon be removed because of one small area of concern. Like the very first doctor on my case at the other hospital, my new doctor informed me that they would only need to surgically remove the area of the colon that had the hole in it, and that I may not need a colostomy bag at all.

Compared to the option of having my entire colon removed, this news came as somewhat of a relief. So once again, I mentally prepared myself for surgery and was ready to just get it over with. Then, a day or so after I was admitted to the new hospital, I was listening to a song by Alvin Slaughter, called *Anything*, and the words to the song say *"God can do anything, everything and anything. There ain't nothing He cannot do...He can do anything but fail."* While I was listening to the song, I heard God ask me the question, *"Do you really believe that?"* My knee-jerk response was *"Of course I do God."* Then He asked, *"Will you trust me?"* At that point I was getting nervous and thinking, *"Where is this going?"* It was then that I got a very heavy impression from the Lord that I was to refuse the surgery and trust that God would miraculously heal my colon and close this hole.

I told my husband what I heard from the Lord, and he joined his faith with mine and we proceeded together in telling the doctors that I was refusing the surgery, against medical advice. Needless to say, the doctors were perplexed by my decision and strongly advised that I reconsider, but I stood on what I heard from the Lord. Their response was *"Mrs. Morgan, holes in the bowel do not just close on their own."* Despite the medical facts, I stood on the truth of what I heard from the Lord.

In order to prove their point, they insisted that I eat something and stated that they would release me from the hospital with their blessing if I did not experience any severe abdominal pain as a result. Now up to that point, I had not eaten in thirteen days, as I was being fed intravenously for the purpose of bowel rest. Nevertheless, I was given a regular hospital menu and encouraged to eat anything off of the menu, which included items such as hamburgers and spaghetti. Any other time I had been placed on bowel rest for a long period of time, I would transition to clear liquids first, then full liquids, bland and soft foods, and then a regular diet. That transition usually takes one to two weeks. But the doctors were on a quest to show me that I was making the wrong choice in refusing this bowel resection, so I made the entire transition in a matter of an hour.

I'll never forget that meal as long as I live. I chose a tuna fish sandwich, the softest item I could find on the menu. I said the longest blessing over that food that I had ever said in my life. I took very small bites at a time, wondering whether or not my stomach was going to explode. Members of my potential surgical team would come into the hospital room every ten minutes to see how the food was digesting. After several minutes, to my relief and the doctors surprise, I had absolutely no pain or adverse effects from eating the sandwich at all!

As promised, the doctors released me from the hospital that night, asking me to schedule an x-ray and a follow-up appointment with my doctor in two weeks to confirm that the hole was really gone. I did just that, my doctor reviewed my films and confirmed that the hole had disappeared! That was over nine years ago, and I still have not undergone that particular surgery.

What a journey! It began with a doctor telling me that they were going to remove my entire colon, and ended with God closing the hole Himself, with no need for surgery at all. However, I would have experienced a totally different outcome if I had not discerned and obeyed the voice of God when He impressed it upon me to refuse the surgery. I am a living witness that discernment is key in possessing what God has promised you.

As we return to the story of Samuel, in verse 8, *"Eli realized that the LORD was calling the boy."* It took someone older and wiser to serve as the means in which Samuel would learn the voice of God. Please note that sometimes, it takes one with experience in hearing the voice of God to lead the younger generation to The Voice. This bedside scene speaks to the importance of spiritual mentors or guides. It took someone else more mature and experienced, to listen, realize, and advise Samuel. Without Eli, he would not have understood that it was God who was calling him.

The Lord called to Samuel a fourth time, indicating God's persistence and insistence on having His way with him. God would not let Samuel or Eli get a good night's sleep until Samuel responded back to God *"I'm listening."* God is still looking for us to respond to Him in the same manner Samuel did. *"Lord, I'm listening."*

God has always chosen to risk the distortion of His Word by using humans as His messengers, just as He used the Biblical writers, the Church and everyone who proclaims God's Word to the world today. His desire is that men and women would be spiritually mature partners in the work of salvation. God could have easily spoken to Samuel clearly and directly, but that would not have cultivated his maturity. God calls us to exercise our spiritual discernment, and in so doing, we become open to things that go beyond the rational, and consider what is seemingly impossible in the natural.

Questions for reflection:

Can you distinguish the voice of God from others, including your own?

Do you have a mentor in your life that can help you in discerning God's voice?

Day 11
Position Yourself for God's Provision

Your present location must accommodate your future destiny. In other words, you must position yourself in a place where the blessing is going to come. God has a set place for you to receive all of the provision you need to fulfill your divine purpose. In the very beginning, God created the garden and then planted Adam there. Let's take a look at a story in 1 Kings 17:1-4 (NKJV) in which God demonstrates the importance of proper placement.

> *And Elijah the Tishbite, of the inhabitants of Gilead, said to Ahab, "As the LORD God of Israel lives, before whom I stand, there shall not be dew nor rain these years, except at my word." Then the word of the LORD came to him, saying, "Get away from here and turn eastward, and hide by the Brook Cherith, which flows into the Jordan. And it will be that you shall drink from the brook, and I have commanded the ravens to feed you there."*

Up to this point in the Bible, there is no mention of Elijah; he kind of just pops up on the scene. Elijah was the first in a long line of prophets that God sent to Israel and Judah. Israel, the northern Kingdom, had no faithful kings throughout history. Each king was wicked, leading the people in worshipping pagan gods. There were few priests left, because most of them had gone to Judah, and the priests appointed by Israel's kings were corrupt and ineffective. Therefore, God called prophets like Elijah to try and rescue Israel from its' moral and spiritual downfall.

In this passage, people were worshipping Baal because they thought this false god brought the rains and the harvests. But Elijah boldly confronts King Ahab, a Baal worshipping king and prophesies that except by his word, there would be no rain for several years. God uses Elijah to be a part of the message to Israel, just like He wants to use your life, calling and positioning to be a part of His message to the church, your region, and to this nation.

Although God used Elijah to predict the famine, the prophet was still affected by his own prophecy. However, God gave Elijah clear instruction as to what to do during this time. A famine is a drastic shortage which leads to starvation and hunger. Just as God spoke to Elijah, He wants to talk to you during your time of famine – whether it be a shortage of finances, health, peace or otherwise, so listen for His voice.

The Lord tells Elijah to GO to Cherith, for He had commanded ravens to feed him THERE. In essence, God was saying to Elijah that in order for him to survive the drought, he was first going to have to move from his present location. Many of us are dying in our respective famines because we refuse to heed the Word of God when He tells us that it is time for us to GO. The fear of the unknown, like the fear of failure, has the power to paralyze us along our journey towards destiny. However, we have to trust that if God is telling us to GO, He must have a THERE already prepared for us.

Back to the text, we see that God gave Elijah a directive as to where he should move. God assured Elijah that when he moved, he would drink of the brook Cherith and be fed by ravens. In a nation that was required by law to care for its prophets, it is ironic that God would use ravens to provide for Elijah. Ravens are unclean birds and known to be creatures that are takers rather than givers. The lesson to be learned here is that God has help for you where you least expect it. He provides in ways that go beyond our narrow, limited expectations. But, you must be in position for the provision.

God was saying to Elijah, if you go to the right place, supernatural provision will show up. I've heard it said that divine supply follows divine placement. If Elijah had been at any other place, he wouldn't have been fed by ravens. God has your place of supernatural provision. He has a place called "there" prepared for you, but you must follow His leading.

Continuing on in 1 Kings 17:7-9 (NKJV):

> *And it happened after a while that the brook dried up,*
> *because there had been no rain in the land. Then the*
> *word of the LORD came to him, saying, "Arise, go to*
> *Zarephath, which belongs to Sidon, and dwell there. See,*
> *I have commanded a widow there to provide for you."*

Just when Elijah had gotten comfortable with the provision by the brook, it dried up. Sometimes God dries up your "brook" to drive you back to your source, which is Him. We can fall in love with the "handouts", and forget that God is the source of our supply. The ravens, nor the brook, weren't Elijah's source but rather God's method of provision. We must make sure that we don't get married to a method or anchored to a memory of what God has done in the past.

When the Holy Spirit wants to do a new thing, we have to get away from the way He performed the miracle before and embrace His new plan in a new place. God tells Elijah to GO to Zeraphath for He commanded a widow to provide for him THERE. Once again, the prophet had to GO, so that He might find His new place of provision.

You must discern the place of God's blessing for your life. If you insist on staying where you are, then you're going to miss the provision that God has for you THERE. For example, you may be in the wrong place of employment. You don't want to work in just any field. Therefore, pray for discernment that will lead you to a place where you have favor with your employer. In Ruth 2:2 (NKJV), Ruth expressed her desire to her mother-in-law Naomi pleading *"Please let me go to the field and glean heads of grain after him in whose sight I may find favor."* The place God has for you will be a place of influence, favor, and prosperity.

Sometimes, the set place God has for you won't appear to be prosperous at first. When Ruth initially found the right field to work, she only labored in a corner of it. However, she was promoted from working in that insignificant corner to owning the whole field. Ruth found favor with Boaz, and they eventually were married. She started out as only a worker in the field and ended up as the owner. But it started with her being in the RIGHT place.

Are you in the right place, or are you determined to stay positioned in a place which God has told you to leave? God often closes one door, opens another, but we allow ourselves to get stuck in the hallway.

As I look over my life's journey, I realize that I would have forfeited my destiny if I allowed myself to get trapped in a place that was no longer God ordained in my life. As I've mentioned previously, God called my husband and I out of the church in which we first met. We could have easily stayed there where it was familiar and never ventured out for fear of the unknown. Unfortunately, we would have missed our Kingdom purpose which was to shepherd a flock and impact the hundreds of lives that have come through our ministry. It started with stepping out on a Word from God that said it's time to GO, because He had prepared a place called THERE for us.

Like Elijah, we were comfortable at the next place that God sent us after we left our first church home. But then, the "brook" dried up, that church closed, and we were forced to seek God's direction for our next place of provision, which we would eventually find in the form of our ultimate calling, Restoration Station Christian Fellowship.

If you know that you are in your set place of God's provision, I urge you, don't leave it! However, if you're not THERE, don't stay where you are another day longer than you have to. If you will obey God's GO, you will find His THERE for your life.

Questions for Reflection:

Are you stuck in a place in which God has "dried up"?
Do you need to conquer the fear of the unknown?

Day 12
Discipline Your Way to Destiny

The difference between who you are and what you want to be is what you do. I've heard it said that *"There is no elevator to success, you have to take the stairs."* Fulfilling your dreams requires perseverance, hard work, determination and DISCIPLINE.

Self-discipline is the ability to make yourself do what you should do, when you should do it, whether you feel like it or not. Self-discipline is similar to perseverance - the hard work you do after you're tired of doing the hard work you've already done. Discipline gives you the ability to control your impulses, emotions, desires and behavior. It is being able to turn down immediate pleasure and instant gratification in order to gain the long-term satisfaction and fulfillment that comes from achieving higher and more meaningful goals.

Yet, it is often challenging to focus on long-term benefits when we are in the midst of experiencing short-term discomfort. Exercise and schooling are great examples of this point. They both can be extremely grueling in the process and require intensely focused effort in order to reap the rewards that are to follow.

Discipline is the bridge between your goals and accomplishment. You have to learn how to focus your mind and energies on <u>your goals </u>and persevere until they are accomplished. When you are disciplined, you are able to reach your goals in a reasonable time frame. This type of self-control requires that you cultivate a mindset whereby you are ruled by your deliberate choices rather than by your emotions, bad habits or the influence of others. The disciplines you establish today will determine your success tomorrow.

However, it takes more than just willpower for lasting self-discipline. It takes a power greater than yourself. 2 Timothy 1:7 (NLT) states that *"God has not given us a spirit of fear, but a spirit of power and love and self-control."* God wants you to develop the level of self-control that pushes you to do things, even when others are giving up. I have noticed that successful people are disciplined people.

Those who exemplify self-discipline:

1. **Control their moods**. Disciplined people are not moody and live by their commitments, not their emotions. *"A man without self-control is as defenseless as a city with broken-down walls"* (Proverbs 25:28, LB).

2. **Master their mouth**. A dear family friend always used to say, *"A lie is never to be told, but the truth is not always to be heard."* In other words, one who uses self-control should think before they speak and determine if what they are about to say is beneficial or detrimental to the hearer. In other words, *"He who guards his lips guards his life"* (Proverbs 13:3, NIV).

3. **Are not easily provoked**. I once heard a pastor say in his sermon that a man is as big as the things that make him angry. How much can you take before you lose your temper? *"If you are sensible, you will control your temper. When someone wrongs you, it is a great virtue to ignore it"* (Proverbs 19:11, GNT).

4. **Keep a schedule and stick to it**. If you don't determine how you will spend your time you can be sure that others will decide for you! *"Live life then, with a due sense of responsibility ... Make the best use of your time..."* (Ephesians 5:15–16, PH).

5. **Manage their money wisely**. Dave Ramsey puts it this way, "Live like no one else, so you can live like no one else." The disciplined learn to live on less

than what they make and invest the difference. *"The wise have health and luxury, but fools spend whatever they get"* (Proverbs 21:20, NLT).

6. **Take good care of their health.** *"Good health is not something we can buy. However, it can be an extremely valuable savings account"* (Dr. Anne Wilson Scaef). Disciplined people understand that they can accomplish more and enjoy their achievements when they are in good health. *"...each of you should learn to control your own body in a way that is holy and honorable"* (1 Thessalonians 4:4, NIV).

The more you accept God's control over your life, the more self-control He gives you! A great example of exemplary self-control and discipline is the story of Joseph found in Genesis chapters 37-50. Joseph's brothers were jealous of him because he was the favorite son of his father Jacob. Jacob also made a beautiful coat for Joseph *"a tunic of many colors"* (Genesis 37: 3, NKJV). When the brothers saw the coat *"they hated him and could not say a kind word to him."*(Genesis 37:4).

Joseph relays two of his dreams to his brothers. In the first dream he recounts how he and his brothers were binding sheaves of wheat and while Joseph's sheaf stood tall, the brothers' sheaves bowed down to it. In the other dream, *the "sun and <u>moon</u> and eleven stars were bowing down to me."* (Genesis 37: 9) These dreams were prophetic but no one knew it at the time. Nevertheless, the brothers were insulted by the dreams, and Jacob was upset by them as well.

Joseph's brothers planned to kill him and throw him into a pit saying that wild animals had devoured him. Reuben, the firstborn, urged his brothers not to kill Joseph, therefore Judah came up with the idea of selling Joseph to some Ishmaelites for twenty pieces of silver. Joseph is then removed from the pit and sold.

The brothers kept Joseph's coat of many colors, killed a goat, and dipped it in the goat's blood. They lied to their father Jacob saying that they found the bloodied and torn coat to make him believe that Joseph had been killed.

Meanwhile, the Ishmaelites traveled to Egypt and sold Joseph to the household of Potiphar *"one of Pharaoh's eunuchs, the captain of the guard."* (Genesis 37: 36, KJV). *"The Lord was with Joseph and he prospered."* (Genesis 39: 2, KJV) Eventually, Joseph found favor with his master, and he became his personal servant and *"his master put him in charge of his household and entrusted him with all that he had."* (Genesis 39: 4, KJV)

Potiphar's wife kept trying to lure Joseph to sleep with her. Joseph was an honorable man and did not betray his master. Potiphar's wife tried one last time to get Joseph to bed by grabbing his cloak but he ran away, leaving his cloak in her hands. She falsely accused Joseph of trying rape her and Joseph is then thrown in prison. Even in prison, *"The Lord was with Joseph and gave him success in everything."* (Genesis 39: 23, KJV) Consequently, Joseph became a supervisor of the other prisoners.

Sometime later Pharaoh became offended by his butler and baker, so they were thrown in jail. Joseph became responsible for them and helped them to interpret their dreams. The baker was hanged and the butler got his job back, just as foretold in a dream interpretation that Joseph had given them. The butler forgot all about Joseph until about two years later.

Pharaoh had a dream but no one in his court could interpret it. That's when the butler remembered that Joseph, who was still in prison, had accurately interpreted his dreams. He then informed Pharaoh who immediately summoned Joseph. Joseph interpreted Pharaoh's dream as a vision of the future where there would be seven years of plenty followed by seven years of famine. When Joseph suggested to put a wise person in charge of food management, Pharaoh gave him the job. Joseph became second only to Pharaoh and began laying aside crops for the famine.

When the famine came *"the whole world came to Egypt to buy corn from Joseph..."* (Genesis 41: 57, KJV), including Joseph's brothers. They didn't recognize Joseph and he made them go back to Israel to get their brother Benjamin, Joseph's closest brother. Upon their return with Benjamin, and after an emotional meeting, Joseph reveals his identity and they share a tearful reunion. The sons return to Israel to get Jacob so he can reunite with his long lost son.

Here are some lessons of self-discipline that we can learn from the life of Joseph:

1) He never did anything that damaged his character.

2) He always told the truth, no matter what potential trouble it could have caused.

3) He never responded to hate (he was not easily provoked).

4) He stuck to his calling without considering his own comfort.

5) He didn't respond negatively to ridicule (he mastered his mouth).

Joseph learned to have faith in the fact that God had a much larger purpose in all the troubles he encountered in his life. Joseph submitted to all of the injustices and unfair treatment inflicted upon him in order to serve God's fuller purpose, even though he didn't know what that purpose was during the process. Joseph's self-discipline ultimately led him to his destiny, and his dreams were fulfilled.

What his brothers meant for evil, God meant for good. We are reminded through the life of Joseph that all things work together for good to them who love God and are called according to His purpose (Romans 8:28). Short-term gratification is not worth forfeiting destiny. Joseph had plenty of opportunities to lose his temper, let his emotions get the best of him, say things that he may have regretted later, but he exhibited self-control from the pit to the palace, and consequently God allowed him to fulfill his calling, even though it was several years in the making.

Your dream, with all of the twists and turns that you may experience from conception to manifestation, is worth the wait. I encourage you today to exercise discipline in your life, even through your trials and tribulations, so that you may possess your purpose and accomplish your God-given goals.

Questions for Reflection:

What areas in your life could you exercise more discipline in?

Do you have control over your moods?

Are you able to master your mouth?

Do you keep a schedule and stick to it?

Do you manage your money wisely?

Do you take good care of your health?

Day 13
Destiny is a Decision Away

"What should I do?" We ask ourselves this question every day of our lives. It may take on different forms such as, *What should I wear this morning? Which route should I take to work today? What am I going to have for dinner?* Simple decisions that we make repeatedly don't necessarily have ramifications that will impact our lives or destiny. However, there are decisions that have effects and consequences that ripple through eternity.

We are where we are today because of a decision we made yesterday concerning everything such as our marital and family status, finances, and our health. Our decisions are important! I'm sure if you had it to do all over again, somewhere along the way, you would have done some things differently, and made better choices.

A wrong decision leads to a bad habit. A bad habit leads to a loss of control. Loss of control ultimately leads to bondage. For example, someone may decide to take drugs initially for recreational use. That recreational usage of drugs may lead to a drug habit or addiction. The drug addiction can then lead to a life that spirals out of control because of their inability to function without them.

There is no need to pray about certain decisions because they are ungodly or unbiblical. For example, a decision as to whether or not you should date someone who is married requires no deliberation. Likewise, whether or not you should rob a bank doesn't require prayerful consideration. The answer is clearly no in both scenarios. The Bible provides definitive direction as to what to do in these cases. *"Thy word is a lamp unto my feet, and a light unto my path."* (Psalm 119:105, KJV) The Ten Commandments in the Bible are not ten suggestions. They are understandable and clearly intended by God to show His people what to do and what not to do.

The Word of God is given not to constrain you, but rather to protect you. A practical example would be the enforcement of a speed limit. Speed limits are not put into place because the government wants to prohibit drivers from experiencing the joy and adventure of driving fast. These motor vehicle laws are put into place with the intention to improve road safety and reduce the number of casualties from traffic collisions.

God has instituted laws and standards, not to limit our fun and enjoyment, but rather to protect us and those around us from the casualties that can and will occur when we transgress His laws. Satan works hard to influence our choices, knowing that when we make the wrong turn on the pathway to purpose, it has the potential to delay our destiny or cause us to miss it altogether. 2 Corinthians 11:3 (NIV) states, *"But I am afraid that just as Eve was deceived by the serpent's cunning, your minds may somehow be led astray from your sincere and pure devotion to Christ."*

The enemy of your soul wants to dim your light, and take away your effectiveness as God's witness. When you've sinned or missed the mark in the sight of God, the devil will use that as a tool to make us feel that we are no longer worthy to be used by God. But the devil is a liar, and even when you have messed up, your biggest mess can be used as God's greatest message to bring Him glory and honor.

On the pathway to your purpose, I want to caution you to stay away from snakes who can influence you to make the wrong choices in life.

In Genesis 3:1-7, Satan first appears as a serpent.

"Now the serpent was more cunning than any beast of the field which the LORD God had made. And he said to the woman, "Has God indeed said, 'You shall not eat of every tree of the garden'?" And the woman said to the serpent, "We may eat the fruit of the trees of the garden; but of the fruit of the tree which is in the midst of the garden, God has said, 'You shall not eat it, nor shall you

touch it, lest you die.'" Then the serpent said to the woman, "You will not surely die. For God knows that in the day you eat of it your eyes will be opened, and you will be like God, knowing good and evil." So when the woman saw that the tree was good for food, that it was pleasant to the eyes, and a tree desirable to make one wise, she took of its fruit and ate. She also gave to her husband with her, and he ate. Then the eyes of both of them were opened, and they knew that they were naked; and they sewed fig leaves together and made themselves coverings."

Snakes have the following characteristics that are shared by people who are influenced by the devil:

1) They are cold-blooded; Beware of those who are cold, calloused and lacking compassion for others.

2) They adapt to all kinds of environments; those who the enemy may use to detour you on the road to destiny can appear to become acclimated with the church, or your family in an effort to gain proximity to you so that they may easily influence you.

3) They are deaf and partially blind. Snakes can't hear, so they sense ground vibrations and they have difficulty seeing still objects, so their prey is usually on the move. In other words, "snakes" usually attack those who are doing something and headed somewhere.

4) Use poison to kill their prey. As we see in verse one of this passage in Genesis chapter 3, the serpent poisoned Eve by trying to get her to question the Word of God, when he told her, *"You shall not surely die."* This is a deadly tactic of the enemy. When we begin to negotiate what we know we heard

from the Lord, we are headed for disastrous results.

We often make wrong decisions based on the lust of the eyes (it looks good), lust of the flesh (it smells and feels good), and the pride of life (it makes one feel special, or better than someone else). Unfortunately, we also often get others involved in our wrong choices, like Eve involved Adam. Unfortunately Eve's wrong decision affected Adam, and ultimately mankind.

We also discover from this passage that wrong decisions can cause you to hide from God. Adam and Eve, realizing they were naked, tried to hide their shame with fig leaves. People are still using fig leaves to hide their shame, and God is asking some people the same question He asked of Adam, *"Where are you?"* When people become ashamed of their ungodly lifestyle, they stop attending church, discontinue praying and no longer allow themselves to be used by God. Consequently, they get kicked out of their respective "gardens", or out of God's presence and His perfect will for their lives.

There are some choices that we need to make in life that are neither right nor wrong; they just require wisdom and Godly insight through prayer. Here are some criteria that may help you in your decision-making process.

Make sure you can ask God to bless your decision.
Your decision should be something that you can take before the Lord with a good conscience and ask Him to put His stamp of approval on. For example, God cannot bless a dating relationship in which one or both of those involved are married to someone else. *"The blessing of the LORD makes one rich, and He adds no sorrow with it."* (Proverbs 10:22, NKJV)

Your decision should be glorifying to God.
Would your decision be something that would honor the Lord? Ask yourself how the Lord would be lifted up or blessed by your plans. If you are presented with a lucrative opportunity that would cause you to break one of God's

commandments, that opportunity is not for you. *"...whether you eat or drink, or whatever you do, do all to the glory of God."* (1 Corinthians 10:31, NKJV)

Your decision shouldn't be a stumbling block.
Make sure your decision doesn't negatively affect the lives of your Christian brothers and sisters. Even if you don't feel it's wrong, it may offend or harm the sensitive faith of those who don't share your convictions. For example, taking a job as a bartender may be offensive to others who don't believe that Christians should drink. *"...beware lest somehow this liberty of yours become a stumbling block to those who are weak."* (1 Corinthians 8:9, NKJV).

Your decision shouldn't hinder your life.
Your decision shouldn't be something that would weaken your Christian life or influence you towards disobedience. It should edify and build you up in the Lord, not tear down your confidence in the strength and power of God. For example, if your potential new job opportunity would prevent you from attending church on a regular basis, you may not want to take that position. *"...let us lay aside every weight, and the sin which so easily ensnares us, and let us run with endurance the race that is set before us."* (Hebrews 12:1, NKJV).

Make your decision to please God, not man.
You should seek to make decisions that bring pleasure to God, not to appease others. For example, if your family is pressuring you to get married, but you know that you're not ready for that level of commitment, do not get married just to make them happy. *"And whatever you do, do it heartily, as to the Lord and not to men."* (Colossians 3:23)

Consider the consequences of your decision.
There are consequences to every decision, both good and bad. Be sure that you consider the long-term ramifications you would have to face as a result of your decision. God is merciful, so He will forgive sin and poor judgment, however

you still may have to live with the results of your decision for the rest of your life. *"Do not be deceived, God is not mocked; for whatever a man sows, that he will also reap."* (Galatians 6:7, NKJV)

Ask yourself, *"Would I want to be doing this when Jesus returns?"*
If Jesus cracked the sky while you were operating in your decision, would you be embarrassed or delighted? Would His presence make you comfortable or ashamed? *"Therefore you also be ready, for the Son of Man is coming at an hour you do not expect."* (Matthew 24:44, NKJV)

Seek the Lord about it.
When we consult the Lord in prayer, He grants us wisdom and direction. Remember, God will never tell us to do something that contradicts His written Word. *"In all your ways acknowledge Him, And He shall direct your paths."* (Proverbs 3:6, KJV) *"There are many plans in a man's heart, Nevertheless the Lord's counsel; that will stand."* (Proverbs 19:21)

Seek Godly counsel or advice.
Ask the advice of those who live Godly lives and have a good track record of Christian experience and wise decision making. Do not seek the counsel of those whose walk with the Lord is questionable or who have experienced repeated failure in making sound decisions. *"Where there is no counsel, the people fall; But in the multitude of counselors there is safety"* (Proverbs 11:14, NKJV). *"Blessed is the man who walks not in the counsel of the ungodly..."* (Psalm 1:1, NKJV)

Decision making is a very important part of the journey towards success. It requires discernment, wisdom, prayer and Godly counsel. Adam and Eve would never have been kicked out of the garden if Eve wasn't talking to the serpent in the first place. You must be careful as to who you allow access to your ear gates, as they will influence your decision-making. Remember, one wrong turn while on course towards your destiny can delay the fulfilment of your dreams and aspirations. However, if you follow God's path for your life, your destiny may be only one good decision away!

Questions for Reflection:

What major decisions have led you to where you are in life today?

Can you identify any possible "snakes" in your life?

Which of the above criteria should you start implementing in your decision-making process?

Day 14
Embrace the Season You Are In

Scripture tells us that God sets the times and seasons of our lives. Solomon, the wisest man that ever lived said in Ecclesiastes 3:1, *"To everything there is a season and a time to every purpose under the Heaven."* In Genesis 8:22 (KJV), it says that *"While the earth remaineth, seedtime and harvest and cold and heat, and summer and winter and day and night shall not cease.* Daniel 2:20-21 (KJV) says, *"Praise be to the name of God for ever and ever; wisdom and power are his. He changes times and seasons...."*

You can't change time. No matter where you are in the world, one minute equals sixty seconds. The word "times" that we find in this verse in Daniel is actually the Greek word "chronos", which is a period marked by years, months, weeks and days. We find a form of "chronos" in the word, "chronometer", an instrument that is used to tell time, like a watch. Another word in which we find a form of "chronos" is in the word "synchronize", which means to cause or occur at the same time. For example, my church is "synchronized" to assemble for worship at 9:00 am.

The word "seasons" in this verse of Daniel is "kairos", which means the right, opportune or supreme moment. "Kairos" is the appointed time in the purpose of God when He acts. There is a Biblical illustration of a "kairos" moment in John 5:4 (NKJV). *"For an angel went down at a certain season into the pool, and troubled the water: whosoever then first after the troubling of the water stepped in was made whole of whatsoever disease he had."* The kairos moment in this verse is the certain season in which the angel would trouble the water. It wasn't a scheduled date on a calendar, but a moment in time in which God would move by troubling the water.

While "chronos" time is quantitative, a kairos moment is qualitative and spiritual in nature. A kairos moment is not an exact demarcation of time. In the northeast of the U.S. where I live, we experience all four seasons in their true and purest form. However, just because summer is marked on June 20th of the calendar doesn't mean the temperature won't go up to 85 degrees on May 31st. Spiritual seasons or kairos moments can begin and show up unexpectedly in our lives, just as summer-like conditions may show up without any warning in the springtime.

Here are some important things to remember about spiritual seasons:

1. You can't schedule or change a season. Seasons are implemented by God and remain under God's control. In Acts 1:6, the disciples asked Jesus if He was about to restore the kingdom to Israel and He replied. *"It is not for you to know the times or seasons the Father has put in His own authority."* (Acts 1:7, NKJV) In the natural, there will always be winter, spring, summer, fall. No matter how much you desire the season to change, you have to just wait it out. Likewise it is the same within the spirit realm. Sometimes there are seasons in our lives that we can't wish or pray our way out of. It is what it is until that season is over.

2. However, we can change and adapt to the season that we are in. Adaptability is the ability to adjust to new circumstances. Therefore, if it is winter time, get a winter coat. If it's autumn, rake the leaves that have fallen to the ground. In other words, instead of railing against the season you're in, make the proper adjustments so you can survive it.

3. Every season requires a change, whether it be a change in attitude, direction, vision, goals or relationships. God may have you in a certain season in life so that He can provoke you to change a mindset that cannot go with you into your destiny.

4. Every season has a purpose. Get in the habit of asking God, *"What are you trying to teach me in this season?"*

5. Seasons are entered into and left, based upon key events that take place. For example when you end a relationship or lose a job, it's a catalyst for a new season to begin. What you may be perceiving as a crisis, may be God's way of ushering you into a new season and one step closer to your real purpose in life.

As a personal example, a bad bout with Crohn's Disease caused me to leave my job where I had worked for several years. As I mentioned in the beginning of the book, I had gotten to a point in my position in which I had reached the proverbial "glass ceiling". I was feeling stuck, and had come to realize that my career was not my calling. I knew God had more for me to do than what I was currently doing at my place of employment. However, I had become comfortable and complacent on my job due to the decent and steady paycheck.

But at some point, I got so sick that it was difficult to go to work on a consistent basis. I eventually had to leave on disability. As challenging as that season was for me physically, it was the catalyst that God used to transition me into full-time ministry, which I have since discovered is my God-ordained purpose.

Seasons, specifically challenging ones, have a purpose in your life and are often used by God to teach you valuable lessons for your ultimate calling. The struggle you are in today is preparing you for the strength you will need for tomorrow and the presence of a storm does not mean the absence of God. Begin to discern the time and season you're in right now, and let God speak to you in and through it. You may discover that it's a divine setup to get you to your date with destiny.

Questions for Reflection:

How would you describe the season that you're in now?

What major life event(s) led you to your current season?

How can you better adapt to the season that you're currently in?

What changes do you need to make in your attitude, direction, vision, goals or relationships as a result of your current season?

What may God be trying to teach you in this season of your life?

Day 15
Don't Despise Divine Frustration

Have you ever stepped out on what you believed was a Word from God, and somewhere in the middle of the process, you questioned whether or not you really heard from Him? This questioning of our spiritual discernment often comes when our step of faith does not yield the outcome that we expected. Perhaps you have been in this situation before, or you are experiencing it right now. If so, I want to propose to you that you may be encountering a supernatural setup or what I call, *"divine frustration"*.

This very thing happened to Jesus at the onset of His ministry as described in Mark 1:9-13:

> *"At that time Jesus came from Nazareth in Galilee and was baptized by John in the Jordan. As Jesus was coming up out of the water, he saw heaven being torn open and the Spirit descending on him like a dove. And a voice came from heaven: "You are my Son, whom I love; with you I am well pleased." At once the Spirit sent him out into the desert, and he was in the desert forty days, being tempted by Satan. He was with the wild animals, and angels attended him."*

When God gives you a word, expect something to show up to test that word, and it's not always the devil, sometimes it's God in the form of divine frustration. In such cases, the Lord will tell you what to do and then orchestrate opposition.

There will be times when the Spirit of God will lead you into a fight, or a wilderness experience, so that He may be glorified and your enemies know that He is the true and living God. A biblical illustration of this can be found in Exodus 14, when Moses and the children encountered the Red Sea. The backdrop to the story is that God appointed a man named Moses to deliver the children of Israel out of Egypt and out of slavery. God hardened the heart of Pharaoh, ruler of Egypt, causing him not to release the

Israelites. Consequently, God sent ten plagues to the Egyptians, which led him to fear God and finally release them from captivity. Then, God hardened his heart again, and the Egyptians pursued the Israelites while they were fleeing from Egypt. God then gives instructions to Moses, informing him that He was going to use their enemies so that He may be glorified.

God chooses what we go through, but we choose HOW we go through it. The children of Israel started to murmur and complain about their dilemma, and we often do the same. Instead of grumbling about the challenge we are facing, we should ask God what He's trying to say to us through this situation. Find out what lessons He wants us to learn and where He wants us to be at the end of the process.

In Exodus chapter 14:13-18, God declares to the children of Israel that the enemies they were facing, they would see no more. He asked Moses why he was crying about their situation, and let him know that this wasn't a time for lamenting but rather a time for progress. The Lord then gives Moses a strategy for their deliverance. When you are encountering divine frustration, this isn't the time for you to weep, it's the time for you to move forward. Listen for God's voice. He has a plan for you to get you out of your mess that will ultimately bring glory and honor to God.

At this point, the Israelites had the Red Sea in front of them, mountains on both sides and Egyptians following close behind. It appeared as though God had led them to a dead end where they would be overtaken by their enemies. God tells Moses to stretch his rod over the Red Sea. Miraculously the sea parted and they were able to walk safely through on dry ground. As the Egyptians continued in pursuit of the Israelites, God once again told Moses to lift his rod. The Red Sea returned to its full depth causing Pharaoh's army to drown.

Sometimes, God will turn up the heat in your life in an effort to burn up anything that is not like Him. This heat has a way of motivating you to make some necessary changes needed for your divine purpose. God knows there are some things we won't do, fix, or adjust if we aren't under pressure. We shouldn't have a problem with pressure, once we recognize it is God who's putting it on us. We must trust and believe that He won't put more us than we can bear. He will give us the strength to endure the process and He won't leave us to handle the weight alone.

God uses these types of situations to build your faith. The things He has in store for you to do in your future are going to require a level of faith that you don't have right now. Therefore, He is going to orchestrate some supernatural setups to show you that all things are possible with God. He's going to deliver you out of some seemingly impossible situations so that you can witness His miraculous power.

It is also important to note, that God used what Moses already had in his hand to bring about his freedom from bondage. You may want to pray and ask God what you already possess that can be used as His instrument for your deliverance. For example, if you are experiencing a financial drought, God may want to use this season in your life to take inventory of the giftings, skills and abilities that you possess, which could lead to a stream of income for your household. An old English proverb says that *"Necessity is the mother of invention."* In other words, sometimes difficult or impossible scenarios in your life may prompt inventions or creative ways to reduce the difficulty. That financial lack you're experiencing now, may lead to a new invention or a start of a business that could eventually lead to your wealth and prosperity.

The story in Exodus chapter 14 ends with Moses and the children of Israel gaining the victory over the Egyptians. I want to let you know, that your story will also end victoriously. If you are living upright before God, but experiencing turmoil in your life right now, you may be experiencing divine frustration. Rejoice, knowing that your season of divine frustration is not a punishment, but rather preparation for your promotion.

Questions for Reflection:

What experiences in your life can you describe as "divine frustration?"

How has God used divine frustration to build your faith?

What lessons can or have you learned through God's supernatural setups?

Day 16
Keep it Moving

Genesis 11:31-12:5 (NIV)

"And Terah took his son Abram and his grandson Lot, the son of Haran, and his daughter-in-law Sarai, his son Abram's wife, and they went out with them from Ur of the Chaldeans to go to the land of Canaan; and they came to Haran and dwelt there. So the days of Terah were two hundred and five years, and Terah died in Haran.

Now the LORD had said to Abram: "Get out of your country, from your family and from your father's house, to a land that I will show you. I will make you a great nation; I will bless you and make your name great; and you shall be a blessing. I will bless those who bless you and I will curse him who curses you; and in you all the families of the earth shall be blessed." So Abram departed as the LORD had spoken to him, and Lot went with him. And Abram was seventy-five years old when he departed from Haran. Then Abram took Sarai his wife and Lot his brother's son, and all their possessions that they had gathered, and the people whom they had acquired in Haran, and they departed to go to the land of Canaan. So they came to the land of Canaan."

On Terah's way to Canaan, he came to Haran and got stuck in a land in which he was only supposed to be passing through. On the road to destiny, we must be careful not to lose sight of our ultimate destination. There are times on the pathway to purpose, it is necessary to makes some rest stops in order to refuel for the rest of the journey. However, we should never turn a temporary situation into a permanent circumstance.

For example, you may have to get a part-time job for extra income to help pay for the schooling necessary to accomplish your goals. While you're in that part-time position, be sure to constantly remind yourself that working there is only TEMPORARY. It is a means to an end. Don't make the mistake of getting so comfortable with extra income such that you quit school and remain in a dead end job that is not your calling.

I know people who intended to purchase a home but needed to rent an apartment until they were able to save enough money for the house. They lost sight of their goal and eventually found themselves content living in an apartment. The apartment was only supposed to be a stop gap.

Then there's the individual who dated someone who they knew was not marriage material. However, they entered into the relationship to cure their loneliness. Years later, they couldn't walk away because they felt they had invested too much of their time and energy into the relationship. Therefore, they settled for someone that was never God's perfect will for their lives.

When people choose to settle at "Haran", the land in which they were only supposed to pass through, they may die there, unfulfilled, having never reached their original destination. If you're stuck in what was only supposed to be a means to an end, get up and get moving!

When Terah died in Haran, notice God speaks to Abram and tells him to pick up where his father left off. The lesson here is, if you don't fulfill your destiny, God will raise up another to do what you were supposed to do.

I am reminded of when Esther debated with Mordecai as to whether or not she was going to go before the king to plead on behalf of her people. She was fully aware that in so doing, she would risk being put to death by the king.

Mordecai replied in Esther 4:13-14 (KJV),

> "...*Think not with thyself that thou shalt escape in the king's house, more than all the Jews. For if thou altogether holdest thy peace at this time, then shall there*

enlargement and deliverance arise to the Jews from another place; but thou and thy father's house shall be destroyed: and who knoweth whether thou art come to the kingdom for such a time as this?"

As you may be tempted to settle for less than God's best while in your pursuit of your destiny, I ask you the same question, *"How do you know whether you have come into the Kingdom for such a time is this?"* You have been uniquely created to fulfill a unique assignment in this season. However, if you don't do it, God will raise up another, and you and your house will suffer as a result.

Back to Abram, the first thing God tells him is that he was to depart from his country, his family and father's house. In other words, the Lord was saying it was time to get out of his comfort zone. God wanted him to step out of the familiar and put his total trust in Him. God is saying the same thing to us. If we are going to do anything great for God, we have to be willing to step away from the familiar so that God can do a new thing in and through our lives. The will of God is always going to stretch you outside of your comfort zone.

Why does He want you to move out of the familiar? Because He wants to make your name great, and make you a blessing like He did Abraham. If you are going to experience the new you, you must be able to discern the voice of God, believe the Word of God, and then act on it. I've heard it put it this way: Belief is a conviction of a truth and obedience is acting on that truth. Your destiny is tied to acting on the truth of what you heard.

We also learn from this story that it's never too late to pursue your purpose. Abram was seventy five years old when God told him to proceed towards his destiny. No matter what stage of life you're in, God still has a plan for your life. Listen for God's voice, and when He tells you what to do, obey immediately. Remember, delayed obedience is disobedience.

I caution you today not to get stuck in a place in which you were only meant to pass through. If you are trapped in what was only meant to be a temporary circumstance, I pray that God would give you the courage to break free from anything that has you bound, and keep it moving!

Questions for Reflection:

Have you gotten stuck in any area of your life that was only supposed to be a temporary circumstance?

If so, what action step are you going to take TODAY to start moving forward again?

Day 17
Count it All Joy

I have experienced some very challenging circumstances throughout my life's journey. I have suffered from a debilitating, inflammatory disease for more than half of my life. This condition has been accompanied by many painful flare-ups and several hospital stays over the years. My health condition has caused me to discontinue working a full time job, which at times, has severely impacted my household's finances. As a result, we've been on the brink of foreclosure, homeless and forced to live with family, and have even had a car repossessed.

It has been my desire to bear children but I have experienced years of infertility and multiple miscarriages. I still have yet to experience the joy of bringing forth a child into this world. Words cannot express the heartbreak and disappointment that has surrounded this issue of my life.

As a pastor, I have experienced many of the occupational hazards that come with the position – being falsely accused, people leaving the church in offense and bearing the weight of the responsibility of shepherding a flock.

However, as Andre Crouch penned it, *"through it all, I've learned to trust in Jesus, I've learned to trust in God...through it all I've learned to depend upon His Word."* In other words, I've learned to COUNT IT ALL JOY!

James 1:2-3 says:

> *"My brethren, count it all joy when you fall into various trials, knowing that the testing of your faith produces patience."*

In this life, you are going to face or *"fall into various trials"*. The first command in this passage of scripture is to *count it all joy*. The word "count" actually means "to consider". You *consider* with your mind and thought processes, not with your feelings. This verse is not saying to FEEL joyful, but rather to THINK joyfully in your trials. How do you consider it all JOY? By leading your mind toward the right biblical perspectives. You reflect on the providence of God, His love, the ministry of the Holy Spirit, and the promises of His Word. Take all of that into consideration as you face your various trials and tribulations. Joy, in its purest form, does not just happen. It takes a deliberate act of your will. It reminds me of what the psalmist says in Psalm 34:1 (KJV), "*I will bless the Lord at all times: His praise shall continually be in my mouth...*" We may not always FEEL like blessing the Lord, but it must be an act of our will to do so, because He's worthy of our praise.

The Merriam – Webster dictionary defines joy as a feeling of happiness that comes from success, good fortune or sense of well-being. But for the spirit-filled believer, joy has a much deeper meaning that is not predicated on external things. I love Pastor Ed Young's definition of joy as described in his book *"Outrageous, Contagious Joy"*:

> *"Joy can be defined as the positive confidence I possess by knowing and trusting God regardless of circumstances. Joy is inner delight derived from an intimate relationship with Christ."*

This definition given by Ed Young is much different than the one provided by the dictionary. A joy that is based on happiness, is circumstantial. However joy from a biblical and spiritual standpoint is relational, based on our connection to Jesus Christ. Therefore, the book of James is conveying to us that nothing we go through should shake the trust and confidence that we have in our Lord and Savior Jesus Christ.

With all of the challenges I've faced throughout my lifetime, I have been able to stay on the pathway to purpose because of my relationship with Jesus Christ. Please don't get me wrong, there have been times when I wanted to quit and give up on my dreams and aspirations, but that "inner delight" would kick in and not allow me to throw in the towel. Why? Because the *"joy of the Lord is my strength"* (Nehemiah 8:10). It's that strength that has allowed me to continue my destiny journey when my flesh felt it couldn't go on any further. Jesus is and has been the source of my joy, producing the strength I need to keep going.

Trials come upon us, as unexpectedly as the ringing of a phone. It is absolutely inevitable that in the course of our daily living we are going to bump into these times of testing. Christians, no matter how godly they may be, are not exempt from being "enveloped in trials".

Think about Job in the Bible. God bragged on him to the devil, saying *"there is no one on the earth like him; he is blameless and upright, a man who fears God and shuns evil."* (Job 1:8, NIV). Yet, God allowed the devil to take his family, property and even his health. However, God told the devil he could not take his life. It is important to note that God is in control of the degree of hardship we experience at every stage of our life.

In the natural, it is nonsense to consider our trials joy, so God must have a very profound explanation as to why we should. The first reason given to us in James is that the trial He allows is testing our faith.

I ran across a paper written and produced by Microsoft that discussed the need for testing as it relates to setting up an e-commerce website on the internet. The document included this definition of testing that I found to have great spiritual relevance.

> *"Testing is the process of running a system with the intention of finding errors. Testing enhances the integrity of a system by detecting deviations in design and errors in the system. Testing aims at detecting error-prone areas. This helps in the prevention of errors in a system. Testing also adds value to the product by conforming to the user requirements (studying to the test)."*

Anything that is considered valuable or important is tested. I'm sure you have come to appreciate that items we use on an everyday basis are tested before we operate or consume them. For example, manufacturers of pharmaceutical drugs conduct clinical trials to ensure they are safe, accredited and do what they claim that they will do. Utterly trivial things are not tested. Since the Lord considers us to be precious to Him, He subjects us to all kinds of trials. He does this in an effort to put our faith under all kinds of pressure in different circumstances.

Test and trials are also used to develop perseverance, maturity and fulfillment. The test is an exercise, and every exercise strengthens. Troops go out on military exercises to become tougher men and women. A young athlete runs for longer and longer distances, to prepare himself for the marathon race. His exercises produce endurance. A student takes a 'mock' exam so that he or she is not ill-prepared when the real exam comes.

Paul says it in Romans 5:3-4 (KJV), "*we also rejoice in our sufferings, because we know that suffering produces perseverance, perseverance, character, and character, hope. And hope does not disappoint us, because God has poured out his love into our hearts by the Holy Spirit, whom he has given us.*"

Bridges often have signs of the load limit they can bear. Trucks carrying heavier loads are forbidden. Likewise, God knows what load we are able to bear. It is God who puts the load on us, and He knows our breaking point. "*There hath no temptation taken you but such as is common to man: but God is faithful, who will not suffer you to be tempted above that ye are able; but will with the temptation also make a way to escape, that ye may be able to bear it.*" (1 Corinthians 10:13, KJV)

God has placed a different load limit on each of us. He won't allow us to carry more than we can bear. No Christian is exempt from trials of any kinds. The one guarantee is that if we put our trust in God, our faith will not fail. Therefore, do not interfere with God's plan for your life when you go through a trial by running from it. Don't give up on your marriage when you encounter conflict or disagreement. Don't give up on pursuing your college degree when it gets challenging. Don't forfeit your ministry when you encounter opposition. Endure the testing so that your faith may be mature and complete.

In closing, I encourage you to remain in the presence of the Lord, for in His presence is the fullness of joy, according to Psalm 16:11. How can you get into the presence of God? Through prayer, reading His Word and praise and worship. As you practice these spiritual disciplines you will find yourself abiding in the presence of God on a consistent basis. Consequently, you will be surrounded by the joy and strength you need to face every trial that will come as you continue on in this trek towards fulfilling your God given dreams.

Questions for Reflection:

Have you had the proper perspective concerning the tests you've faced over your lifetime?

Do you spend enough time in the presence of God so that you can properly endure your trials?

Day 18
Run Your Race

I remember when I was as a child, my babysitter, Mrs. Brown, would give lunch to all of the children under her care, while telling each child, *"keep your eyes on your own plate."*

Perhaps she was simply trying to keep the peace amongst a bunch of rambunctious kids, but within her famous phrase hid a deeper revelation. It doesn't matter what the person next to you has on their plate, eat what's in front of YOU.

I was always tempted to look around to compare my plate with everyone else's plate. I wanted to see what everyone else was eating, to make sure that no one else got more potato chips than I did, or had something that looked tastier than what I was served.

In this game called life, I've had to learn to run MY race. How my "plate" compares to someone else's doesn't matter. It's my plate to eat. What I didn't realize back then was Jane couldn't have the peanut butter and jelly sandwich I had because she was allergic to peanuts, but Jane would have killed to have my sandwich. Johnnie's plate looked different than mine because he brought his lunch from home so his mother could ensure he wasn't eating too much sugar because he had diabetes. Mrs. Brown didn't serve me as many potato chips because I was notorious for wasting them because I got full quickly. There was a reason why our plates didn't look the same, but Mrs. Brown's point was that it was none of each other's business.

The same can be said of our respective "plates" today. We are often tempted, like I was at the babysitter's, to see what God has served up to those around us. We measure our own success by the perceived success of someone else around us. It may look like someone else has been given a better meal, metaphorically speaking. However, they can't handle the type of food I can, and while I'm jealous of their meal, they may be secretly jealous of mine. So often, the thing we take for granted is the very thing someone else is praying for.

There are times when we feel like someone else has been given more food to eat, and that God has served us up a small plate. But God's portions are distributed based on what He knows you can handle.

Then there's the issue of comparing ourselves to something that isn't real in the first place. In this day and age of social media, people know how to present a fake image for the sake of looking good in front of the world. After several years of counseling married couples and mentoring women, I've coined the following phrase, "Don't judge a person's life by their Facebook cover". Folks let you see what they want you to see, and hide all of the rest under a mask. I've left a counseling session on more than one occasion shocked and absolutely amazed. You would NEVER know what's going on in people's marriages or personal lives based on how they present on social media.

You may have heard it put this way, the grass looks greener on the other side, but it's AstroTurf. However, if we would be committed to cutting and watering our grass, we too would have a beautiful "lawn" with REAL grass.

The habit of comparison is destroying our society. Unfortunately, we often use comparison as a ruler and assess our own value based on someone else's victories or failures. Consequently we will beat ourselves and others down with the measuring stick of comparison.

Christian author, Ann Voskamp wrote the following in a blog:

> *"Comparison is a thug that robs your joy. But it's even more than that — Comparison makes you a thug who beats down somebody – or your soul.*
>
> *Scales always lie. They don't make a scale that ever told the truth about value, about worth, about significance. And the thing about measuring sticks, girl? Measuring sticks try to rank some people as big and some people as small — but we aren't sizes. We are souls. There are no*

better people or worse people — there are only God-made souls. There is no point trying to size people up, no point trying to compare – because souls defy measuring."

When we constantly compare ourselves to others, we are operating in pride because we are taking the focus off of God and putting it on ourselves and others. We are telling God that what He created isn't good enough and we know what's best.

What do the scriptures have to say with regards to comparison?

Galatians 6:4
"But let each one examine his own work, and then he will have rejoicing in himself alone, and not in another."

1 Thessalonians 4:11-12
"that you also aspire to lead a quiet life, to mind your own business, and to work with your own hands, as we commanded you, that you may walk properly toward those who are outside, and that you may lack nothing."

1 Timothy 6:6-7
"Now godliness with contentment is great gain. For we brought nothing into this world, and it is certain we can carry nothing out."

Psalm 139:14
"I will praise You, for I am fearfully and wonderfully made; Marvelous are Your works, And that my soul knows very well."

Exodus 20:17
"You shall not covet your neighbor's house; you shall not covet your neighbor's wife, nor his male servant, nor his female servant, nor his ox, nor his donkey, nor anything that is your neighbor's."

Remember, we were created with a purpose to fulfill a specific calling. We are uniquely flawed in our bodies, personalities, and abilities. What we perceive as flaws are God's handiwork to be used for His honor and glory. Therefore, we should not waste time or energy comparing ourselves to anyone else. If we compare ourselves to anyone, it should be God Himself. Ephesians 4:13 (NKJV) says, *"till we all come to the unity of the faith and of the knowledge of the Son of God, to a perfect man, to the measure of the stature of the fullness of Christ."* We should seek to use God as our measuring stick for what is right and good. So therefore, as it states in Hebrews 12:1, *"let us be sure to lay aside every weight, and the sin which easily entangles us"*, including the weight of comparison. Let us run with endurance, the race that is set before US, and not the race of another.

Questions for Reflection:

Have you been guilty of comparing yourself to other people?

What do consider to be your personal flaws?

How might those flaws be used to glorify God?

Day 19
Change is A Process

Having read the previous chapters of this devotional, you have probably discovered by now that change is necessary on the pathway to purpose. However, we must realize that change is a process, not an event. When we see a caterpillar turn into a butterfly or watch the winter give way to spring, we understand that change is a process. While we are on the roadway to destiny, waiting to achieve our dreams, we often fall into the trap of perceiving change as an event. By understanding and managing change as a process, we will be more successful when helping individuals and ourselves.

A biblical illustration of the process of change in Mark 8:22-26 (NKJV):

> *"Then He came to Bethsaida; and they brought a blind man to Him, and begged Him to touch him. So He took the blind man by the hand and led him out of the town. And when He had spit on his eyes and put His hands on him, He asked him if he saw anything. And he looked up and said, "I see men like trees, walking. Then He put His hands on his eyes again and made him look up. And he was restored and saw everyone clearly. Then He sent him away to his house, saying, 'Neither go into the town, nor tell anyone in the town.'"*

First, I want you to notice that people brought the blind man to Jesus. This miraculous healing was initiated by those around, begging the Lord to touch him. Today, there are many people around us who are spiritually blinded and in need of healing. I believe that God wants you to be a change agent, like those who brought the blind man to Jesus. I challenge you to identify those around you that are blind and in need of a touch from Jesus. Ask God how He can use you and your calling to be a facilitator of the change of others.

There are three states of change, as illustrated in this story.

Joseph has a dream that he would rule over his family. Before this dream came to pass, Joseph was thrown into a pit and was also imprisoned. He had to fight for his survival from the pit to the palace.

God told Moses he was going to lead His people out of Egypt, but he first had to fight Pharaoh and his army before they were delivered from bondage.

God spoke this prophetic Word over Joshua's life in Joshua 3:7, *"Today I will begin to exalt you in the eyes of all Israel, so they may know that I am with you as I was with Moses."* After that declaration, Joshua had many enemies, and was forced to fight many battles with his adversaries.

While Jesus was being baptized by John the Baptist, God Himself spoke from Heaven saying *"This is My beloved son, in whom I am well-pleased".* (Matthew 3:17, KJV). However, He was immediately led into the wilderness where he fought against the temptations made by the devil while fasting forty days and forty nights.

The greater the prophetic promise, the greater the adversary, which means the bigger the fight. It's important to keep our faith strong during these times of waiting. *"Fight the good fight of faith. Take hold of the eternal life to which you were called when you made your good confession in the presence of many witnesses."* (1 Timothy 6:12, KJV)

I encourage you to fight for your prophetic promise in the right realm. In other words spiritual warfare should be fought in the spirit. *"For we do not wrestle against flesh and blood, but against principalities, against powers, against the rulers of the darkness of this age, against spiritual hosts of wickedness in the heavenly places."* (Ephesians 6:12, NKJV)

Then, we should take the right weapons to the fight. *"For though we walk in the flesh, we do not war according to the flesh. "For the weapons of our warfare are not carnal but mighty in God for*

101

pulling down strongholds." (2 Corinthians 10:3-4). Our spiritual weapons are the Sword of the Spirit which is the Word of God, prayer, and praise and worship. Jesus fought the devil in the wilderness with the Word of God. I challenge you to declare the Word of God and speak life during every demonic attack. Warfare praying is necessary to break through the power of resistance of the enemy to release the power of God. Praise is a weapon of mass destruction. God dwells in your praise, therefore the enemy has to back up!

I declare that you are a champion. You have a fighting spirit and you are anointed to finish your race. *"However, I consider my life worth nothing to me; my only aim is to **finish the race** and complete the task the Lord Jesus has given me —the task of testifying to the good news of God's grace."* (Acts 20:24, NKJV)

I encourage you not to just finish the journey, but to FINISH STRONG. *"Do you not know that in a race all the runners run, but only one gets the prize? Run in such a way as to get the prize."* (1 Corinthians 9:24, NKJV) I pray that your testimony would be that of Paul who said in 1 Timothy 2:4, *"I have fought a good fight, I have finished my course, I have kept the faith."* Fight for your destiny, finish the race, and finish strong!

Questions for Reflection:

Have you had any prophetic dreams or visions? Write them down (Habakkuk 2:2)

Have you had anyone prophecy over your life concerning your divine purpose(s)? Write them down.

Do you believe your destiny is worth fighting for? If so, why?

Have you been fighting in the right realm with the right weapons?

Day 21
Don't Look Back

We are on the last day of our journey together on this roadmap to destiny. You've come so far now, having made a deliberate decision to embark on a journey towards your calling. You are a big thinker who has embraced the process of change and are committed to doing whatever it takes to get to your destination. However, you can forfeit all that you've learned and experienced over these last twenty days if you choose to look back longingly at where you came from. It may be tempting to do so because the pathway to purpose is admittedly a challenging one. There are many twists and turns, as well as bumps and bruises, but they are all worth it when you consider the grand future that lies ahead of you.

Life is filled with defining moments. You may only have a handful of them in an entire lifetime. They are life's forks in the road, where choices regarding your destiny are made. A biblical example can be found in the book of Ruth. In chapter 1, Naomi's sons died, and she presented both of her daughters-in-law Orpah and Ruth with the same opportunity to go back and return to their homes of origin. Orpah took her up on that offer. However, Ruth moved forward with Naomi to Judah where she would ultimately meet and marry Boaz. God ordained Boaz to be a significant part of Ruth's destiny, as Jesus would eventually come through their lineage. Orpah, on the other hand, is never heard of again from that point on in the Bible. What if Orpah had NOT turned back? Perhaps her life would have been different and the Bible may have had more to say about her.

Sometimes life presents you with moments in which turning back is extremely tempting. These are moments that can define you and your family for a lifetime or for generations to come. These temptations may come in the form of an old habit, a friend from your past that drags you back to an old life, an old career path that was comfortable but not your calling, an old mindset, or an old environment that was not conducive for your destiny to be fulfilled. Full-time ministry and entrepreneurship has been hard and unpredictable for me at times - financially and otherwise. I have often been tempted to look for a full-time position in the engineering field or college administration in an effort to bring some stability to my life and my pocketbook. Every time I consider walking away from what I know God has called me to, I immediately become depressed at the very thought. My life may be frustrating and unstable at times, but I know it's what I've been graced and purposed by God to do. God has confirmed through circumstances that He does not want me to go back to my old career path. There have been a few times in which I've made actual steps back to a steady nine to five position, and every time, I've gotten too sick to keep the job, or sick before I even take the position. When God says don't look back, He means it!

Remember the story of Sodom and Gomorrah in Genesis chapter 19? God burned the city down because of its wickedness, but in His grace and mercy allowed Lot's wife to escape from being killed in the destruction. However, Lot's wife looked back and turned into a pillar of salt. The Hebrew for "looked back" means more than to glance over one's shoulder. It means to regard, consider or pay attention to. God punished her for regarding and considering the place that God deemed wicked, so He caused her to be stuck in that place.

Like Lot's wife, if you continue to look back at what God has rejected for your life, you too can get stuck there, frozen in time. My husband often bumps into old classmates who only talk about the glory days of having the best high school football team in the region or the fun they had as teenagers. It's like they have been frozen in time, seemingly not having done anything significant with their lives since high school.

We cannot turn back and secretly long for the lifestyle we once had before He saved us. We must put all of that behind us and move away from it. That's what tripped up the Israelites after they were delivered from Egypt. While they were in the wilderness they longed to go back to Egypt, their place of bondage again. Jesus reminds us in Luke 9:62 that *"No one who puts his hand to the plow and **looks back** is fit for service in the* *kingdom of God."* That mindset of the Israelites was one of the reasons none of the millions of adults who were a part of the Exodus, other than Joshua and Caleb, entered the promise land.

We have to avoid becoming paralyzed by the past, otherwise we can become spiritual paraplegics. Spiritual paraplegics are those who are unable to move forward due to fear of an unpleasant history repeating itself gripping our souls. We may consider giving up on the dreams that God has put in our hearts because of a traumatic life event. I encourage you not to dwell on the past, but rather take its lessons and move on.

> *Not that I have already attained, or am already perfected; but I press on, that I may lay hold of that for which Christ Jesus has also laid hold of me. Brethren, I do not count myself to have apprehended; but one thing I do, forgetting those things which are behind and reaching forward to those things which are ahead, I press toward the goal for the prize of the upward call of God in Christ Jesus"* (Phil. 3:12-14, NKJV).

Have you ever noticed that the windshield of your car is bigger than your rearview mirror? There's so much more to see and consider in front of you than there is behind you. You will never find your destiny in your rear view mirror. On this quest towards your ultimate pursuit of destiny, I leave you with these final words. Keep moving forward and don't look back!

Questions for Reflection:

Have you been tempted to turn around on this road to destiny? If so, why?

Is there a traumatic life experience that has put the fear of moving forward in your heart?